What do I do now :

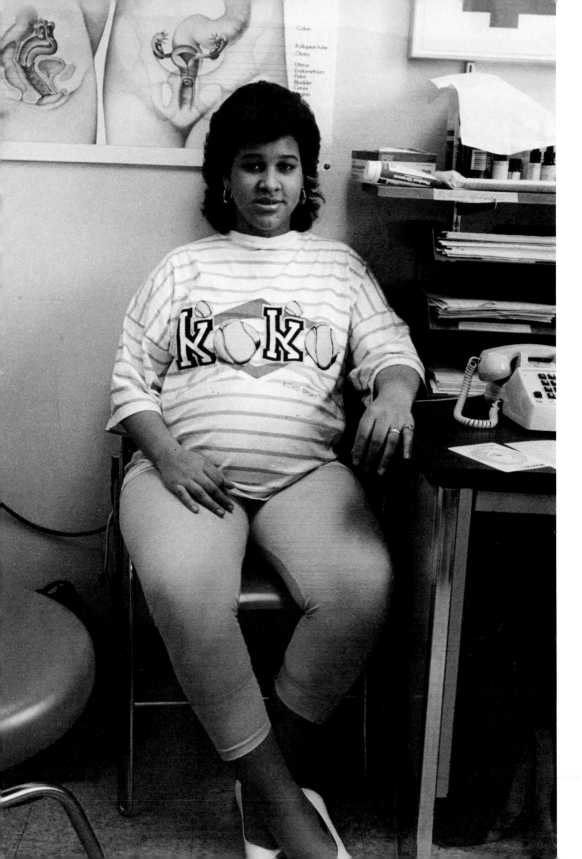

What do I do now?

Talking About Teenage Pregnancy

Susan Kuklin

G . P . P U T N A M ' S S O N S

New York

For Refna Wilkin

G. P. Putnam's Sons, a division of The Putnam & Grosset Book
Group, 200 Madison Avenue, New York, NY 10016
Published simultaneously in Canada.
Printed in the United States of America

Book design by Joy Taylor

Library of Congress Cataloging-in-Publication Data
Kuklin, Susan.
    What do I do now?: talking about teenage pregnancy/Susan Kuklin.
    p. cm.
    Summary: Discusses the many decisions and considerations faced by pregnant
teens, including the fact of getting pregnant, abortion, prenatal examinations
and care, counseling, and psychological pressures.
    1. Teenage mothers—United States—Juvenile literature. 2. Teenage
pregnancy—United States—Juvenile literature. [1. Pregnancy.]   I. Title.
HQ759.4.K85   1991   90-45775   CIP   AC
362.83'92'0973—dc20
                ISBN 0-399-21843-2 (hardcover)

1 3 5 7 9 10 8 6 4 2

ISBN 0-399-22043-7 (paperback)

1 3 5 7 9 10 8 6 4 2

First Impression

Contents

Introduction

ACCORDING to the Alan Guttmacher Institute, 23.9 percent of U.S. teenage girls will have been pregnant by age eighteen, and more than four out of ten by age twenty. Though these statistics are significant, they do not tell us much about the individuals who make up the numbers. What happens when a fifteen-year-old girl begins to realize that she is feeling nauseous every morning and that she may be pregnant? To whom can she turn? Where can she go? What are her options?

What Do I Do Now? contains first-person accounts by teenagers and their families, talking about unplanned pregnancies, and by the professionals who assist them at four organizations: Planned Parenthood of Bergen County, New Jersey; Metropolitan Medical Associates, Inc.; Spence–Chapin Services to Family and Children (an adoption agency); and The Adolescent Pregnancy Program at North Central Bronx Hospital. Since adoption and abortion procedures and laws vary greatly from agency to agency, and from state to state, the steps I describe are specific for these particular agencies. Where abortion is concerned, regulations are changing. After the second trimester, the right to an abortion is limited. There are exceptions, however—for example, where the health of the mother or the fetus is endangered.

Over a two-year period I interviewed many teenagers who faced an unplanned pregnancy. I found them to be thoughtful, distressed people, coping with heart-wrenching decisions, who were willing to share their stories with others. Many allowed me to accompany them into examining rooms and private counseling sessions. Some were about to have an abortion, while others were still raw from the experience of surrendering their babies for adoption. Still others were dealing with the problems of being teenage parents.

Usually how to deal with an unplanned pregnancy was the first major decision the adolescents had to make. Indeed, it may be the most important decision they ever make. No matter what the outcome, it may well affect them for the rest of their lives. Although the reader may not agree with all the options presented, perhaps the experiences of these teenagers will bring about a more sympathetic understanding of their situations. As Arlene Mayo, the nurse practitioner in this book, put it: "You're damned if you do and you're damned if you don't."

What Do I Do Now? is not a should-you-or-shouldn't-you-have-sex book. Recently headlined political issues, such as a woman's right to an abortion, are not debated either. Moral questions are raised only from the point of view of my subjects and their families. I've tried hard not to proselytize, but there are two exceptions: the need for birth control, and, when the chosen option is to bring a pregnancy to term, for good prenatal care. During some of my interviews, there were times when I wanted to shriek, "You're so smart, why didn't you use birth control!" (I must confess, I did say that on occasion.) There were also times when I met one of my very pregnant subjects walking down a street eating candy and drinking a soda. "Don't eat junk food, eat fruit!" But most of my time with the teenagers consisted of heart-to-heart revelations that often included tears, hugs, and even a few giggles.

Over the course of writing this book there were a number of surprises. I spent many days at Planned Parenthood when no teenage girls asked for a pregnancy test. Most of the women who terminated their pregnancies at Metropolitan Medical Associates were over twenty years old, and many were married. Not all Planned Parenthood affiliates perform abortions, as is the case with the Bergen County medical branch which only makes referrals. Most of the teenage girls interviewed became pregnant by their first boyfriend. Very few of the teenagers used birth control, and most who did used it incorrectly. The notion that black girls have babies and white girls have abortions was unfounded. (Although teenagers from different races were included in every section of the book, I purposely tried to keep racial descriptions out of the narrative unless it was part of a quote. In my view, race is irrelevant to teenage pregnancy.) The pregnant teenager's mother often had a powerful role in determining the outcome of the pregnancy. No one took abortion lightly.

The Ground Rules

As in my book *Fighting Back: What Some People Are Doing About AIDS,* I adopted each organization's confidentiality policy. In cases where "name and identity changed" appears, people's descriptions and locations are deliberately altered in order to protect their privacy. Their experiences, however, are reported exactly as they were told to me. Only those people who chose to raise their babies are photographed for the book. I selected solely those organizations that were open to all the various options available to the pregnant teenager.

How This Book Came About

A number of years ago when I left the teaching profession to become a photographer, my first assignment was to photograph

Appalachian families in Tennessee for Planned Parenthood. I accompanied local outreach workers to remote cabins and small hamlets while they counseled women about family planning and health care. It was an exciting experience that laid the foundation for my career in photojournalism. Years later I photographed Planned Parenthood's annual report. I have always had a great deal of respect for the organization.

At Planned Parenthood Federation of America's offices in New York City, my friend, Susan Newcomer, arranged for me to meet the incoming associate director of education, Maria Matthews. Susan also provided lists of Planned Parenthood affiliates in the area. Every director I called took time out to talk to me about the things teenagers should understand about sex and pregnancy.

I wanted my subjects to be from a wide array of ethnic and socioeconomic backgrounds. Maria suggested that the Planned Parenthood affiliate in Bergen County, New Jersey, would be able to satisfy these criteria. She proposed that I meet Betty Puglisi, who headed its medical division. "You two will be a good match," she told me. She was right.

The Executive Director of the clinic was Bruce Miller. Our first interview began as a simple getting-to-know-one-another, and ended with a frank discussion in which we brainstormed over the various concepts to include in the book. "Don't forget the boys!" Bruce urged. "We have our own sets of expectations, fears, and guilts." Bruce's urging was echoed by my husband, Bailey, who periodically read over my shoulder to be sure that the boys were given a fair hearing. I hope that I didn't let either of them down.

Through Betty and her staff, all of whom made me feel like a colleague, I began to network into the other areas covered by this book. Betty arranged an introduction with Susan Martinelli, who directs the Metropolitan Medical Associates clinic, and she suggested that I call Judy Greene at Spence–Chapin. Everyone at both organizations, from the receptionists to the caseworkers and doctors, was knowledgeable, informative, committed to their work, and friendly. I found them to be infinitely supportive of their clientele, which was their first priority, and supportive of my project. It was a pleasure to work with them.

Susan Stein, a midwife at Planned Parenthood, told me about The Adolescent Pregnancy Program in the Bronx, New York. As far as I know, this is the only adolescent program that includes in one program prenatal care, obstetrics, and pediatrics. Dr. Mutya San Agustin, who started this fascinating program, says, "There are two children to take care of, the child mother and the baby. It is important that the same staff who attends the mother-to-be while she is pregnant continues to take care of the new mother and her baby. We try to provide an atmosphere in the hospital where the mother can take care of her own needs and the needs of her baby." They pursue their mission with warm enthusiasm that is infectious to their patients and me. Something miraculous is always happening.

Many of the teenagers I interviewed could not be included in the book, much to my regret. Various organizations, some of which also could not be featured, provided valuable guidance and information: Planned Parenthood Federation of America, Inc.; the staff and Board of Directors of Planned Parenthood of Bergen County, Inc.; the staff of The Adolescent Pregnancy Program at North Central Bronx Hospital; The Spence–Chapin Services to Families and Children; Manhattan Teen Pregnancy Network; The Sadie American Life Center; Metropolitan Medical Services, Inc.; YWCA Services for Young Fathers; and The Staten Island Teen Pregnancy Network.

Thanks also to the following people: Susan Newcomer, Maria Matthews, Betty Puglisi, Bruce Miller, Arlene Mayo, Patti Niemiec, Brenda Goldston, Dr. Mutya San Agustin, Maude Joseph, Dr. Emelyn Quijano, Sylvia Blaustein, Ileana Hernandez, Leah LaBoy, Susan Martinelli, Dr. Nicholas Poulos, Judy Greene, Susan Lesser, Susan Thomas, Helen Bates, Monica Murphy, Jo Kelly, Hughlett

Powell, James Reynolds, Joey Palermo, Dr. Louise Friedman, Professor Marsha Garrison of Brooklyn Law School, Dr. Martin Goldstein, my husband, Bailey, and my editor, Refna Wilkin.

On a personal note: I am very grateful to the young men and women who agreed to be interviewed. They were open, honest, sometimes illogical, often frightened, yet willing to expose themselves so that others might learn from their experiences. I wish them well and hope that they go on to live happy, fulfilled lives.

S.K.

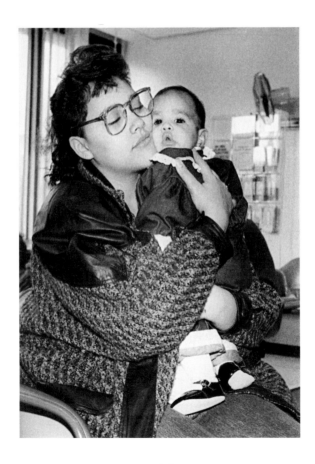

What do I do now?

Lynne with her mother, Peg

1

Lynne and Drew

PAROCHIAL schools on Staten Island, New York, dismiss classes forty-five minutes earlier than public schools. That gave four senior girls, best friends, enough time to drive across the island in a red Le Baron convertible to pick up their other "best friend," Lynne. Lynne's long blond hair, pulled back into a pony tail makes her look even younger than seventeen. She recently transferred to a special public school.

Gazing out the classroom window at her friend's car, Lynne thought back to the days when her biggest decision was whether to buy a blue T-shirt or a pink one. When the bell rang, Lynne was the first one out. It's not that she was afraid that the other students would resent her for her fancy friends in their sleek red convertible, but why take a chance? Once outside, giggling and chatting it up with her friends, she could be a kid again. Pregnancy at seventeen has its problems.

"Shall we hit the mall?" the driver suggested.

"Na, I'm tired," said Lynne. "Just take me home."

Lynne met Drew last year through a mutual friend soon after she broke up with her first boyfriend. At first Drew didn't want a serious relationship. He was pretty popular with the girls and had a reputation as a Casanova. But as time went by, Drew was hanging around Lynne's house all the time. They would kiss on the couch while Lynne's mother, Peg, two sisters, and two brothers sat alongside them watching TV. Peg could tell that this was more than a teenage fling, that they really cared about each other.

Often, the kissing got to be too much for Drew and he would get up and walk out. "I'm not a fool," Peg says. "I could see that he held back for a long time. He couldn't tell her how he felt about her, so he told me."

Because Lynne is extremely shy, every time Drew called she became tongue-tied. During the daily telephone calls, embarrassing silences occurred. Each party prayed that the other one would think of something to say. Say anything! "I use to throw the phone to my mother and they would talk. My mother wanted me to tell him how I felt, but I couldn't. I was afraid of rejection. I was waiting for him to say something."

Peg was well aware that her oldest daughter was about to become sexually active and even talked to her about birth control. "My mother's not stupid," Lynne says. "She knew what was going on." Though Lynne knew about contraceptives, she was too shy to protect herself or to ask Drew to wear a condom. Why didn't Drew use a condom? With hindsight, he says that he wanted Lynne to have his child. That way he would never lose her.

Drew began staying overnight at Lynne's house when her father, a truck driver, was out of town. When her dad was home, Drew slept on the couch in the living room. Sometimes Peg would drive him home early in the morning. When Peg found out that her husband was having an affair with his boss's daughter, the marriage broke up. The week after Lynne's father moved out, Drew moved in, permanently. New sleeping arrangements went into effect. Lynne and Drew moved into her parents' bedroom, while Peg slept on the couch in the living room.

By this time two months had passed without Lynne getting her period. Her mother asked daily, "Did you get it?"

"No."

"Did you get it?"

"NO!"

Eventually Lynne went to her mother's doctor for a pregnancy test. The result of the test was to be given to Lynne over the telephone, but she was afraid to make the call. She asked Peg to call. The doctor would only tell Lynne the results of the test, so reluctantly, she got on the phone. "It's positive," he told her. And then the doctor asked the big question: "What are you going to do?"

"I don't know," Lynne replied, hanging up quickly. Drew, who had been by her side, said, "Oh, no, we're too young." Lynne's mother advised her that she didn't have much time to make up her mind. Lynne called the doctor back and said, "Termination."

As soon as Peg made the arrangements for her daughter's abortion, Drew was told about the plans. He was relieved. Lynne says, "I never wanted an abortion. But when Drew insisted we were too young, I thought, 'Why should I keep it if he doesn't want it?' He was being snotty about everything."

The day before the abortion appointment, Lynne's head was swimming. "I kept thinking, am I doing the right thing? I didn't eat all day because I had had morning sickness. The lady who set up my appointment told me not to eat or drink anything after midnight. By that time the morning sickness had gone so I was hungry and in a bad mood. I couldn't stop crying."

At eight PM, Lynne's mother visited a friend who said, "I don't think you're going to go in the morning."

Peg agreed. "I think she's doing this because of me."

Peg returned home, lay down on the couch, and fell asleep. Drew and Lynne were upstairs trying to sleep. All Lynne could do was cry.

Touched by Lynne's anguish, Drew put his arms around her and said, "Go eat."

"Really?" She looked up at him.

"Yeah."

The couple crept downstairs to tell her mother about the change of plans. Lynne said, "I have something to tell you. . . ." and Peg immediately knew what she was going to say.

"Are you sure?" her mother interrupted. "Do you know what this means?"

"Yeah, I think I'm sure."

Once the decision was made to call off the abortion, new plans had to be made. Drew's mother wanted them to get married while Lynne's mother did not. Peg was afraid they would end up on welfare and never get off it. "I didn't want that for my daughter. I would rather that they took time to get themselves together, mature a little, and then get married. But if they chose to be married, I'd have gone along with it. I want whatever makes them happy."

Drew was without a job. They decided to live together at Lynne's house.

Lynne stopped going to confession. "If the priest asked me if I was having sex, there was no way I would admit to him that I was. Confession would be a waste of time because I would be lying." Many girls in Lynne's crowd at parochial school felt the same way. That's how the friends figured out which of them weren't virgins. Virtually none of them would go to confession.

A pregnant, unmarried Lynne could not return to her Catholic high school for her senior year. Since she was a little girl she had dreamed about going to college and becoming an elementary school teacher, but first she had to graduate from high school. Peg called the New York City Board of Education and explained her daughter's situation. They recommended that she attend The Sadie American Life Center, a public school for pregnant students. There she could finish her senior year, earn a high school equivalency diploma, as well as take courses in prenatal and child care.

"Why isn't Lynne coming to school this semester?" the nuns and her schoolmates' parents asked. "Can the family no longer afford parochial school? Is it because her parents split?" Lynne's friends lied and covered for her. They faithfully met her after school so that she would never feel left out.

Lynne says, "I think my friends were a little embarrassed at first. After all, the next question their parents would ask them was, 'If Lynne is having sex, are you?' My friends would never admit to their parents that they were having sex. Anyway, most parents don't ask. Except my mother. She asked all the time."

After the initial shock, Lynne's friends became excited about the baby, excited that they were going to be "aunts." One asked, "Do you feel pregnant?"

"No, do I look pregnant?" Lynne replied defensively.

Her friends were too curious to back off. "Do you feel fat?"

"Can you feel anything moving inside you?"

"What does it feel like?"

Once Lynne began talking she couldn't stop. "It feels like something else is moving, not me. Late at night it starts moving and moving. It wakes me up. I don't talk to it, but Drew does. He'll kiss my stomach and talk to it." Her friends were fascinated.

Everyone was eager to voice an opinion about what to name the baby. Lynne and Drew made it clear that since they were able to make a baby all by themselves, they could name a baby, too. Drew liked "stuck-up" girls' names like Tiffany and Felicia. Eventually the couple chose Ashley. If the baby was a boy, Drew did not want to give him his name. "Biff or Bleen sounds better," he told Lynne, who wasn't sure whether or not he was kidding.

"I'm not going to name my son Biff or Bleen," she moaned. They had a hard time choosing a boy's name. Drew didn't like most of the names Lynne suggested. Finally, for no particular reason, they settled upon Anthony.

Peg thought her daughter was very lucky. "Years ago when this happened, the girl would be ostracized. Now her friends drop by with toys and other presents for the baby. Her friends' parents are sympathetic. They're glad it's not happening to them."

Living with Drew was not as easy as Lynne thought it would be. The couple fought over stupid things. When Drew was in a bad mood, which became more and more frequent, he wouldn't talk about it. Lynne would ask him what was wrong and he'd snap, "Shut up."

Before long, Drew began going to clubs with his friends, rather than staying at home with Lynne. The clubs are where the girls are, and Drew and his friends were good-looking guys. Peg was upset. Lynne, though she knew where Drew was going, never complained about it. She was convinced that if she did, he would tell her to mind her own damn business.

Peg advised, "Ask! Ask him where he goes. He wants you to ask. He wants you to be a little jealous. He wants to know that you care about him."

Lynne lethargically replied, "I tell him that I love him."

"But you're not as affectionate as you were before you were pregnant."

"He is—all the time," griped Lynne. "He tries to kiss me when I'm watching TV. I yell at him, 'I'm watching something, why are you kissing me? Stop kissing me. Stop touching me.'"

Eventually, Drew resolved to settle down and only go to the clubs once in a while. Lynne, on the other hand, became less resolute. Everything began to aggravate her: her two brothers, her two sisters, and most especially Drew. Before the pregnancy Lynne was shy and retiring; she had since become loud.

As Lynne's due date drew nearer, her thoughts centered more around the baby than Drew and his disposition. She was dying to see what the baby would look like. "Would it be a boy or a girl? Would its eyes be brown, like Drew's, or blue, like mine?"

Drew's thoughts still revolved around Lynne. He sometimes sat around the house doodling, "I love Lynne . . . Lynne and Drew."

Once Lynne began feeling more and more movement, Drew said, "If it moves in the middle of the night, wake me up. Just wake me up." Whenever Lynne awakened, Drew was up, too. "Are you okay?" he'd ask her, touching her belly.

Although Drew is handsome and charming, he tends to put himself down. He did not graduate from high school and he didn't have a job. Lynne would occasionally push him about this. "I know, I know, I have to get a job." Drew was certain that a job would fall into his lap. Lynne complained that she would not be able to go to college, study, and take care of a baby without financial security. "I promise to have a job before the baby arrives," he said, grabbing a jacket to go out who-knows-where.

Lynne's father offered Drew a job driving his truck, but Drew said that he didn't want to get dirty working around trucks. Surprisingly, Lynne and her mother weren't all that concerned. They had faith that Drew would not loaf his life away. Peg said, "There is so much he has to adjust to. Staying home every night with a girl is a big change. He's trying. The responsibilities of fatherhood haven't fully penetrated yet. He's a good kid, he'll come through."

Peg worked, her children went to school, and Drew remained home and kept house. He would not do dishes, but he did everything else. He cooked, emptied the garbage, and vacuumed. He fixed the ceiling and painted the kitchen. He joked that he would be "Mr. Mom."

Lynne was not looking forward to the actual delivery. "I don't want to be wheeled into the hospital. I don't want anyone looking at me during the delivery. I don't want to be in pain. And I don't want to be in a room with some old lady."

She was afraid that she wouldn't know what to do. "I hope it comes out fast. Drew won't be no use to me. He'll be worse than I am."

Lynne's "due day" was Drew's first day driving an upholstery van for an interior decorator. Four days later Lynne still hadn't given birth. She felt lousy. After she drove Drew to work, she returned home to get some sleep before her two o'clock doctor's appointment.

"As soon as my mother and I arrived at the doctor's office, the first telltale sign of the birth came: I started leaking water. It was just a trickle at first. I was scared. Before I could go to the bathroom, my name was called. I prayed that I would not leak while I waited for the doctor in the examining room. But my prayers were not answered. In a matter of seconds, all my underwear was saturated. Even the paper covering the doctor's table was wet. I was so embarrassed.

"When the doctor arrived and saw me sitting there, like a jerk, in my own water, he was totally calm about it. He began to examine me. He could feel that the head of the baby was already down. 'Are you feeling any pains?' he asked me.

"'No.'

"He gave me an internal exam because I was overdue. In the middle of the exam, the rest of my water came gushing out. I was really worried by then, but the doctor was cool, calm, and collected. He said, 'You're going to be a mommy. Now.'

"Oh, my God, I was scared."

Peg, who was in the room holding Lynne's hand during the exam, asked if there was time for them to go home to settle her other kids down. "There is time enough for that but not much more," he said.

Once Lynne told her brothers and sisters about the oncoming event, her sister rushed to Drew's job, shouting, "Lynne's going to the hospital."

Lynne says, "Drew nearly had a heart attack. He hurried home to drive my mother and me to the hospital.

"At the hospital I was prepped, and asked a number of questions: 'Are you on drugs?'

"'No.'

"'Are you allergic to anything?'

1 0

" 'No.'

" 'Have you eaten anything before coming here?'

" 'Yes.'

"The nurse hooked me up to a monitor to watch my contractions, gave me an enema, and put me on an IV. It was unreal.

"Meanwhile, Drew rushed all around the hospital filling out forms and getting my admitting bracelet. He returned to the labor room and, putting on white hospital clothes, sat beside me. My mother stayed outside in the waiting room. Drew's mother arrived about an hour later.

"I wasn't having many contractions the first hour so the nurse gave me medication to induce them. It started to hurt. Drew could actually see a contraction come by watching the line on the monitor. When the line went up, he tried to warn me about what I already knew.

" 'Shut up! Shut up! I can feel the pain,' I yelled at him.

" 'Breathe, breathe, breathe,' he coached me just like he did in the Lamaze classes we went to.

"I couldn't. It hurt too much to breathe.

"By the third hour, we were told that I still wasn't ready to give birth. The nurse asked if I wanted a pain killer. After she gave me a shot, she left to see another patient.

"Drew hadn't had lunch and was hungry. He went down to the cafeteria to eat. Drew's mother thought he should stay with me, and yelled at him, but I was not sorry he left. Once I was alone in the room, I fell asleep.

"When I woke up, the room was spinning. I called the nurse. 'Is the room supposed to spin like this?'

" 'Yes,' she replied.

"For four hours, I was in pain. Thank God, I was only in labor for five hours. I feel sorry for people who are in labor for days. The nurse examined me, and said I was ready to push. She said, 'We'll move you into the delivery room as soon as we can see the crown of the baby's head.'

"The baby hadn't dropped down so she left the room to change into her green delivery gown. Drew, who had come back from lunch, was the only one with me. I pushed and screamed. I felt the baby's head drop further down. I was sure that the baby was coming and the doctor and nurses wouldn't be there to deliver it.

"'The head . . . the head . . .' I shouted.

"And Drew screamed back, 'Shut up and keep your legs closed.' He was afraid that the baby would come out while he was alone with me.

"The nurse returned and said it was almost time. Quickly, she wheeled me into another room, the delivery room, with Drew racing behind us. All I could think about was the pain. As soon as I got into the room, I pushed, three times, and the baby came out. It was a boy. Seven pounds, seven ounces, nineteen and a half inches long, a good-size baby.

"The nurse placed Anthony on top of my stomach while the cord was cut. Then they put a little white cap on his head to keep the heat in. They wiped him off and took mucous from his nose. He was given a bracelet with the same ID that I wore, with my last name, the date, and the time that he was born.

"I looked at him, but didn't really feel anything. I held him for a while and then the nurse gave him to Drew. Drew didn't want to hold him, he was scared. The nurse said that he had to, so he did. Then I held Anthony until the nurse from the nursery took him. When the nurses wheeled me into the hallway, Drew rushed ahead to call our mothers.

"Once I was in my room, my mother visited me for a while. I was glad to see her. I was hungry, but I hated the hospital food. I wasn't very excited. I wanted to put this experience behind me. I wanted to sleep. The following morning I became excited. I couldn't wait for visiting hours. I called everyone, woke up all my friends."

Three days later, Lynne played with her baby all the way home from the hospital. "He's a good boy! He's a good boy! Anthony, are you a good boy?" she sang. Drew drove cautiously to assure his son's safe arrival.

"To Drew, Anthony was a glass baby," says Lynne. "He'd have a heart attack if he thought someone might hurt him. He was even afraid to hold him himself."

Once again the sleeping arrangements were changed. In their five-bedroom home, Lynne's sisters, Erika and Allison, each had their own room, her brothers, Jeremy and Danny, slept in a larger room with bunk beds, and Drew and Lynne kept her parents' room with Anthony in a tiny bedroom across the hall. Lynne's mother continued to sleep downstairs on the couch. She says she actually likes it there.

Lynne says, "Anthony is so little, so fragile. In school I was taught how to wash a baby, but we learned with a doll. It didn't matter how I held a doll. This was different. During the first few months my mother did everything. That made Drew a little jealous. At first, everybody came to see the baby and me. That made Drew more jealous. He complained about every little thing. I told him that he was just jealous, but he insisted that he was not. He said, 'I only want to be alone with you and my son.' In a way he was right. My house is always filled with brothers, sisters, friends, and other relatives. We were never alone."

Every day, when Lynne's brothers and sisters came home from school, they'd go to the crib to pick up Anthony. Friends dropped in and wanted to hold him, even when he was napping. Anthony seemed to like all the attention, but Drew did not. No one asked Drew's permission to hold Anthony, and he took offense.

Lynne says that Drew looked for people to make mistakes with the baby. She tried hard to make people recognize his viewpoint, but no one (least of all Lynne's brothers and sisters) paid any attention to his objections. "The biggest problem was with Drew rather than Anthony," sighs Lynne. "But I love him and I'm happy."

As the weeks passed, Lynne took to motherhood like a fish takes

Lynne with Anthony

to water. She did things that she never expected to do willingly. For example, when Lynne was pregnant she thought that she would be grossed out if the baby dribbled, pooped in his diapers, or made a mush with food. "It doesn't bother me at all. He's mine. That makes all the difference. The only thing that bothers me is that he stares at me when I eat. I hate that."

Lynne's biggest problem, worse than the stares, was getting enough sleep. Like most newborn babies, Anthony did not sleep through the night, so neither could Lynne. Drew did not share this problem, since he never woke up to take care of the baby. Constantly exhausted, Lynne began to resent Drew rather than Anthony.

Peg, Lynne's mother, says, "Lynne was getting no sleep at all, so one night I took the baby. I laid him down beside me in the living room and we both fell asleep. When Drew came home from a night out with his friends and saw me sleeping with the baby, he became furious. He stamped upstairs and awoke Lynne, griping, 'Your mother is taking over. She even sleeps with the baby!' This was the first time that Anthony slept through the night." But Lynne remained awake, fighting with Drew.

After weeks and weeks of constant arguing, Drew told Lynne that the only way they would stop fighting was to find their own place. "Come on, Lynne, we can make it on our own," he said.

"You make $235.00 a week. We can't afford an apartment. I don't want to go on welfare. Until you get a raise or I start making money, we can't touch an apartment. We have no choice but to stay here and put money away." Lynne had always been the more practical of the two.

"The only reason we don't move is because you don't want to leave your mother."

"Well, I wouldn't want to move far away. But a two-bedroom apartment in this neighborhood is about $500. And I want two bedrooms. I don't want Anthony to sleep in the room with us."

The following morning during breakfast, Peg offered a solution.

Drew, Lynne, and Anthony

"You want to get married? Get engaged at Christmas like normal people do. Start saving your money to furnish your home and then, when you can afford it, move out. Find a bedroom set and start paying for it. In about two years, it will be paid for."

"TWO YEARS! ARE YOU NUTS!" Drew exclaimed.

Peg says that Drew doesn't like the bank. He spends his money before he can walk to a bank. When he received his first paycheck, he spent it all on gifts for Lynne: a ring and a gold nameplate necklace that says "I Love You."

By the time Anthony was three months old, Lynne, Peg, Drew, and the brothers and sisters had worked out a routine which allowed them to live together in relative harmony.

Lynne's friends dropped by less frequently than they used to, so Drew had less reason to be jealous. He was no longer afraid of his "glass" Anthony. "He does everything for him. I think he wants the baby to have everything he never had," says Lynne.

"On the weekends Drew does whatever he wants. He simply says, 'I'm going out.' He can leave and I can't. I guess I could if I wanted to, but Drew would be mad. I never go out by myself. Once a week I play bingo with Drew's sisters while Drew baby-sits. Other than bingo, I take Anthony wherever I go."

Lynne's Routine

"Every weekday morning, from seven-thirty to nine, Drew and I take care of the baby. When Drew goes to work at nine, I go back to sleep, while my mother watches him. At eleven my mother goes to work and I get up to feed him. While he is napping, I make his bottles and do his laundry. Baby clothes get dirty very fast.

"Then I clean our room and Anthony's room. Everything takes longer now because when Anthony cries, I stop what I'm doing and go to him. It used to take about an hour to clean the house. Now it takes three hours. I can never put him down. If he cries, I immediately pick him up. When I put him down, he won't stay. If he hears my voice and doesn't see me, he cries. Anthony is so spoiled. If he doesn't get enough sleep, he becomes cranky. I get him to nap by taking him for a drive in the car. When my girlfriends saw how much I must do for Anthony, they said that they will never have kids. My mother heard them and laughed that I should be on TV as an advertisement for birth control.

"I'm about to start college. Drew really doesn't want me to go to school. Education is not important to him. He says that he doesn't want anyone watching the baby except me. I'm going to do it anyway. This is something I've always wanted to do."

Afterword

Anthony, six months old, is a healthy, happy baby. Lynne is a freshman at college. She and Drew broke up. Drew visits the baby regularly and talks to Lynne on the telephone. Once in a while they go out on a date.

Lynne is one of thousands of teenagers faced with an unplanned pregnancy. Her decision to continue her pregnancy was based on her own circumstances, commitments, and values. Other girls choose different options for other reasons. Here are a few. . . .

2

"Now I Have a Big Decision to Make"

IT IS late in the afternoon in the waiting room at the Planned Parenthood medical services of Bergen County, New Jersey. Two teenagers huddle together talking softly. A woman with permed blond hair sits by the window, tapping her foot absentmindedly as she reads a paperback novel. A young man, about sixteen, all alone in the center of the room, wipes his forehead with a crumpled tissue and watches a soap opera on the TV attached to the wall. He wears a stiff, worried smile, but his thoughts seem to be elsewhere.

The plants, magazines, and posters (Balthus, Picasso, Cézanne) help make the room comfortable and cozy. Fresh-cut flowers in the green vase sit on the receptionist's desk. To the right is a bulletin board filled with posters, most of which relate to AIDS:

"Sleep around and you could wind up having more than a good time." "My boyfriend gave me AIDS. I was only worried about getting pregnant."

The medical services provided by this Planned Parenthood clinic include birth control information (including counseling and supplies), pregnancy testing (counseling and referrals), annual exams (pelvic and breast exams, Pap tests, etc.), testing and treatment for vaginal infections, infertility testing, short-term counseling, and AIDS referrals for testing. It does not perform abortions.

Across from the receptionist's desk is the counseling area. Fay Scarlett, in the first office cubicle, is on the phone making appointments and helping with emergency counseling. Today a woman is asking her to confirm an appointment for a pregnancy test. Fay declines, explaining that she cannot confirm appointments over the telephone because it might compromise the confidentiality of the patient. The caller, who is probably not the patient, is furious. Fay is polite, but will not release the information.

In another office cubicle, Carolyn (name and identity changed), 16, talks to Patti Niemiec, a nurse, while her boyfriend nervously remains in the waiting room.

Carolyn claims that she is not worried. Expensively dressed in a short black leather skirt, high heels, black opaque stockings, and an oversize yellow Cashmere sweater, she shakes her head, rearranging long, curly, auburn hair as she tries hard to pay attention.

"Did you watch your cycle?" Patti asks. "Or did you take it for granted that it wouldn't happen?"

"I never missed a period," Carolyn replies. "I was always on time." Then she adds, "I thought I was sterile." Patti looks at her quizzically.

After filling out a medical chart, Patti answers Carolyn's questions about the pregnancy test. The simple laboratory procedure takes about three minutes. A drop of the patient's urine is mixed with a specific chemical reagent. If she is pregnant, the solution will show a distinct reaction. The urine will clump up into tiny, white dots. Otherwise, the urine will remain the same milky solution.

Patti explains, "Regardless of the test result, a pelvic exam is performed to confirm the outcome. If your test is positive, we check the size of your uterus and any softening of the cervix, another indication of a pregnancy, to determine the length of pregnancy. If your uterus is small, it indicates that the pregnancy is recent. If your test is negative, we want to know why you're not getting a monthly period."

Carolyn interrupts, "The thing is, if I am not, I'm going to try to become pregnant. Thinking about this has made me want a baby more and more. I want one. I want to be pregnant.

"Before my boyfriend and I came here we talked about this. I asked him, 'What happens if I am pregnant?' He mentioned abortion. I said, 'Forget abortion. How would you feel about having a baby?' He told me he would want it, but that depends upon how many weeks pregnant I was. I think he wants it."

"Before we jump the gun, why don't you give us a urine specimen to find out if you are really pregnant. We have people to refer you to for help afterwards. Our in-house counselor, Maxine, is a good person to talk to about this if you don't think you can talk to your parents. There's always a way. All right?" They both stand up.

"Yep," says Carolyn, grateful for Patti's arm around her shoulder. She goes into the women's room.

Patti thinks that Carolyn's a lovely girl, and that her boyfriend is probably a decent kid who's saying that he'll help her out because he doesn't want to be a creep. But he's most likely thinking that his family is going to kill him dead when they find out.

In the open space outside the lab, Carolyn waits as Patti performs the test on a few drops of urine. Carolyn says, "I'm nervous. I asked my boyfriend when I last got my period. He didn't remember. All the while I worried, he was calm and cool about it. He said, 'We'll just have to wait and see.' Of course, deep in our hearts we both believe that I can't be pregnant."

Carolyn continues, "I'll be upset if I'm not pregnant, sort of. And I'll be upset if I am. I keep going back and forth. Either way, I'm going to hurt a little bit. Money will be a problem. Neither one of us is good about money. When we have it, it slips right out of our hands. My boyfriend has a job after school and I have an interview at K Mart today. I heard about a woman in Ramsey who takes in pregnant girls. She feeds and clothes them and tries to find them a

The staff at Planned Parenthood Medical Services

job to make them self-sufficient. The girls can't expect to live like Princess Di, wearing designer clothes, but they won't starve or become homeless. That's one possibility if my family throw me out."

Carolyn's test is positive. Patti gives the results of the test to Arlene Mayo, the nurse practitioner, whose responsibility it is to discuss the results of the test, perform the pelvic exam, and counsel the patient about her options.

In the examining room Carolyn undresses from the waist down, neatly lays her leather skirt on a chair, and wraps a white drape sheet carefully around her waist. Arlene knocks on the door, comes into the room, introduces herself, and gently gives her the result of the pregnancy test.

There is no reaction. Finally Carolyn says, "I am very nervous, but I'm not upset. I'm upset for my family. Now I have a big decision to make."

Arlene listens as her patient mutters, "I wanted this. I would have been upset if I wasn't. Now I'm upset that I am." Tears begin to flow as the reality sets in.

Arlene comforts Carolyn and then helps her place each foot in a stirrup at either side of the examining table. As Carolyn leans back, Arlene beckons with her hand. "Come on down here." The patient lets out an anxious laugh and Arlene eases the tension with friendly chitchat.

As they talk, Arlene adjusts a light, and puts on latex gloves. "Now, we're ready to begin the pelvic exam," she says.

The uterus, or womb, is a muscular organ located within the pelvis. During pregnancy, the uterus rises out of the pelvis. Arlene does not examine the embryo, but rather the size of the uterus as it expands with the growth of the embryo. Before doing anything to her patient, Arlene describes how it will feel.

"Okay. You'll feel my fingers touching you. There will be some pressure. There."

A uterus is shaped like an upside-down pear. The lower portion, or stem end of the pear, is called the cervix. It protrudes into the vagina. Arlene puts her fingers into the vagina and feels the cervix.

"I need to feel if there are any changes in your cervix. If it is soft, that's another sign of pregnancy. Now you are going to feel slight pressure. I'm holding the cervix to determine the size of your uterus. Now comes part two. You'll feel a little more pressure."

When Arlene presses her free hand on the girl's abdomen, she can feel the top part of the uterus, so she grasps the entire uterus between her two hands. That's how she determines the size and length of pregnancy.

Arlene talks over the sounds of an air conditioner. The patient becomes silent.

"Okay?" Arlene asks.

"Uh huh."

"Am I tickling you? I just felt your muscle do a nice jump," she says while she continues to work. "Your uterus is still small. Take a deep breath . . . relax."

Arlene reports a five- to six-week pregnancy. "Oh, that's so early," Carolyn sighs. "We have time to talk about it." But the nurse advises that she not wait too long. Her calculations might not be exactly accurate.

Through it all, Carolyn's boyfriend sits in the waiting room watching the soaps. Arlene comes out to get him, while Carolyn gets dressed. Once in the office, holding her hand, he is told the test results. His face flushes and beads of perspiration appear on his forehead. Carolyn doesn't notice.

Arlene says, "You have options and you will have to make a choice. If you wish to maintain your pregnancy, here is a list of hospital facilities that we recommend. If you wish to maintain your pregnancy and place your child for adoption, these facilities will help you with that. If you choose to continue the pregnancy, you must not smoke, drink, or take over-the-counter medications such as aspirin. If you wish to terminate your pregnancy, that, too, is an option." The couple, clearly dazed, try to take in this information. Arlene gives Carolyn a photocopy of the list of all the facilities she just described.

As far as Arlene is concerned, the choice belongs to her patient. Information can be collected from whomever she pleases, but the ultimate decision is hers. "She's the only one who can live in her head," is a phrase Arlene uses with regularity. "Do you have any questions for me?" she asks.

"No," says Carolyn. She seems more at a loss for words than reluctant to talk.

"If you need to talk, I'll be here. But I can't be here around midnight and that's when the reality usually hits the fan. If it gets bad and there's no one to talk to, write it down. Write what you feel. Don't hold back, get it out."

Arlene says, "When you think you might be pregnant, it's one thing. When someone tells you your test is positive, that's a whole new ball game."

Arlene Mayo, Nurse Practitioner

A few years ago, tired of her nursing duties in obstetrics, Arlene sought more stimulating work. In the meantime, a good friend who was a midwife at a teen clinic invited her to do volunteer work there. "Volunteer?" she shrieked. "Give me a break, I've gotta pay bills."

After a while Arlene's curiosity got the better of her and she decided to find out more about the clinic. The director suggested that she volunteer temporarily, and, if she enjoyed the work, they would talk about a paying job. She took it. The teen clinic was fun, different, and rewarding. She enjoyed her dialogues with the teenagers and they readily responded to her counsel.

While there, she learned about becoming a nurse practitioner. "It sounded interesting. Here was a chance to combine counseling and medical skills. But it required an entire year of school, during which I couldn't work. I talked to my husband and daughters. Everyone said, 'Go for it. We'll manage.' And they did."

While Arlene went to school during that year, she cooked the dinners and her husband, Jimmy, took over the marketing, the housecleaning, and responsibilities such as PTA meetings. She slept from nine PM to four AM, studied until six-thirty, and then the day began.

Arlene learned about pre- and post-natal care, physical exams, family planning, complications from pregnancy—everything except the delivery. To work with childbirth Arlene would have to become a midwife, that is, a nurse with additional training in obstetrics to take care of "normal," uncomplicated pregnancies. She was not really interested in deliveries. She cared more about the diagnostic and teaching aspects of her profession. That was nine years ago and she still loves her job.

Arlene talks to her patients about taking responsibility for their actions, but she does not pass judgment on them. Nor does she proselytize. But, once home, she has a lot to say to her own two teenage daughters. Returning recently from an AIDS conference, she threw a bunch of condoms at her two daughters, ages nineteen and sixteen, and announced, "Use these!"

"Ma, please . . ." the older daughter said, nonchalantly, as she lay on her bed reading a magazine.

"Ma, every time you hear about something new, you come home and you try it out on us," the younger one teased. "First of all, we're not about to get pregnant. Gee, we're not sexually active! We're not doing anything to get AIDS."

Nonplussed, Arlene told them that she will never know when they decide to have sex, because they're not going to come to her and say, "Please, Mother, give me some condoms so I can have intercourse." In this family, they are able to talk about sex.

3

"I Better Not
Come Home Pregnant"

IN AN office similar to the one where Carolyn was examined, another patient, Irene (name and identity changed), sits in the waiting area by the lab. An enormous smile fills her face, a symbol of liberation from what she considered the worst thing that could happen in her life. The nurse practitioner just told her the results of her pregnancy test: negative.

"Thank God," she says. "I'm so relieved. I'm usually careful about using contraceptives, but I don't use them 100 percent. The last couple of times I was stupid and didn't use anything. I'm very regular and when I didn't get my period for three months, I was sure that I was pregnant." Irene's words tumble out in a jubilant torrent.

Irene, 16

Irene reports, "I was fourteen when I started having sex. It was weird—I wasn't planning on it. I was with my boyfriend, who was sixteen at the time. We were hanging out at a friend's house. One thing led to another and it just happened.

"I would never, ever talk about sex with my parents. My mother goes to church regularly, but is not really religious. My father is very old-fashioned. Pre-marital sex is a no-no. Eventually, though, my mother found out that I wasn't a virgin when she overheard me talking about it on the phone. She started screaming at me: 'How could you do that!' Then she refused to talk to me at all. After a few days, she couldn't stand the silence in the house. She marched into my room, without knocking, and handed me some religious books about sex. Can you believe that? Obviously, I didn't bother reading what I already knew.

"Finally, she brought out her big-gun threat: my father! I had to promise never to do that 'dirty thing' again or she would tell my father.

"'Yeah, sure,' I promised.

"A few years ago my father said, 'If you ever come home pregnant, you might as well find some other place to live. You won't be living here.' So I thought, 'Well, I better not come home pregnant.'"

Had she been pregnant, Irene would have opted for an abortion. Adoption was out of the question. "I was adopted and that caused many emotional problems for me. I wondered who my real mom was. Why did she leave me? I felt abandoned. Sometimes my mother's family teased me about it. For a long time I wanted to find my birth mother, but now I don't bother.

"I give my adoptive mother a hard time. When she pisses me off, I scream at her that she isn't my real mother. Then I feel bad about saying that.

"When I think about it, I believe that I'd be killing something, but why have a baby who will wind up who-knows-where? These were some of the questions I've been dealing with these last few weeks. I definitely decided that if I was pregnant, I would have an abortion. At my age, having a baby would never work. I'm unfit to be a mother. And if I give birth to it, I would not do to my child what my birth mother did to me." Fortunately for Irene, that is no longer an issue.

A third teenager is not as lucky as Irene. Fifteen-year-old Sue (name and identity changed) arrives at the clinic for a session with the in-house counselor, Maxine, who is trained to work with problems such as hers.

Sue, 15

Sue had been raped by someone she knew. She was too terrified to report it to the police, and then she found she was pregnant as a result. Five months passed before Sue would tell anyone about the rape or the pregnancy. She still would not say who the man was.

Sue didn't know who to turn to. She was deathly afraid that her parents would blame her for the rape and throw her out. When she could no longer hide from the truth, she confided in her brother. Although the family was devoutly Catholic, the brother insisted that she have an abortion. Abortion frightened Sue even more. She was afraid it would be painful, especially since she was well past her first trimester. She was afraid that she couldn't go to confession ever again. She was afraid that she would go to hell. Finally Sue ended up in Maxine's office.

Maxine advises, "You still have choices. But the decision should be based on what is best for you and what would be best for the baby, if you make that choice." Because of Sue's religious background, and the fact that she is so far along into the pregnancy, Maxine brings up the subject of adoption. She explains how the newborn could be placed either immediately after its birth or six months later. If necessary, Maxine would recommend homes where Sue could live until the baby was born.

"Oh, no, I couldn't do that. I couldn't have a baby and just give it away," Sue says, shaking her long, braided ponytail vigorously.

Most of the girls tell Maxine that. If they carry the baby to term, they want to keep it.

"You don't have any time," Maxine warns, speaking to her as if she were her own daughter. Sue starts to cry.

Twenty minutes later, the session over, Maxine walks beside her client into the waiting room, and approaches the brother. Sue does not respond to her brother's questions or to Maxine's hug. She has withdrawn into herself. Eventually, Sue and her brother leave the office. Maxine never learns her final decision because Sue doesn't call back. Although Maxine often thinks about this particular client, she is not allowed to call her because of Planned Parenthood's meticulous commitment of confidentiality.

Maxine says, "Every time I have one of these tough cases, I feel awful. My heart reaches out to these kids."

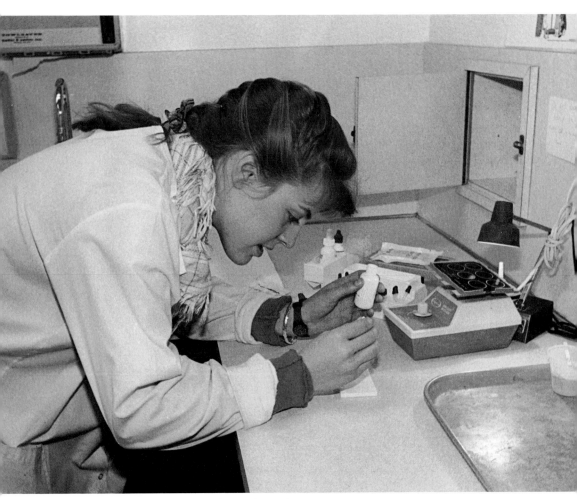

Jennifer Wilson doing a pregnancy test

4

"Just Depend on Yourself"

Tiffany, 18 (name and identity changed)

AN attractive young woman is jittery as she enters an office for her in-take conference, dressed in red jersey harem pants, a white cotton shirt, red leather ankle boots, and black checkered knee socks. Her hair is lightly tinted and slicked back in a velvet barrette. Her makeup is simple and elegant. Heavy gold loop earrings, a chain necklace dangling a gold heart, and a few bracelets complete her carefully composed outfit. In other words, Tiffany is a knockout.

So is her counselor, Jennifer Wilson. The perky college junior introduces herself to Tiffany. An easy rapport between the two young women is quickly established. Their intimate, animated conversation begins with a discussion of hairstyles and where-did-you-find-that-great-skirt.

Jennifer is currently a nursing student at Bergen Community College. When she decided to find a part-time job, her sister-in-law, who works at the Planned Parenthood clinic, suggested that she apply there. "I like talking to people, so when the position of health care specialist became available, I thought it would be more interesting than waiting tables or selling clothes. And it is." On-the-job training took approximately two months. Jennifer's duties include routine in-take questions, weighing, taking blood pressure, and basic testing.

Jennifer gets down to business and explains her role as an in-take counselor. "We're going to do the paper work together and I will explain everything that is going to happen. If you have any questions about anything, including your options, feel free to discuss them with me. Everything here is strictly confidential."

First, they fill out a medical form. Jennifer asks routine medical questions. She learns that Tiffany lives with her father and stepmother, has never had a Pap smear, and that no one in her family has high blood pressure, diabetes, or a stroke. Tiffany's medical chart reveals a visit to this office six months ago for a pregnancy test that was positive. She is back for another one.

Tiffany offers an unsolicited explanation. "The pill made me feel sick. It was like I was pregnant. I was always throwing up and my chest was swollen."

"Did you call to talk to a nurse? Did you talk to anyone?" asks Jennifer.

"No, I didn't. I got my period and then tried the rhythm system. But that doesn't work! I'm so irregular anyway. My boyfriend, Carter (name and identity changed), used condoms, but not every single time."

Sensing that Jennifer is a good listener, Tiffany tells her about the previous pregnancy. "Even though I knew I was pregnant, it took me five months to face it. Finally, when I couldn't deny it anymore, I came here for the test. It was not until I left the clinic that it really hit me. I started crying. I wondered what I was going to do. I had to find a way to have a miscarriage. I was working as a busgirl, carrying heavy things, eating junk food sometimes, worrying all the time. I was sure that I would lose the baby.

"As far as Carter was concerned, this was my problem. He already had a two-year-old child to support and he just started work-ing. Carter's twenty. He's nice but I don't want to stay with him forever. He is not the love of my life. If I had his child, we would be together for a lifetime. I don't want that."

There were no doubts, no discussions. Tiffany knew she wanted an abortion. But she had waited an awfully long time. The longer the pregnancy, the more risk is involved with an abortion. And the more complicated the procedure, the more expensive it becomes. Tiffany didn't know that.

"By now, I hated Carter, couldn't stand him. He wasn't there when I needed him the most. He was going out with other girls. The only nice thing he did was take me to my prom."

What upset Tiffany even more than her philandering boyfriend was the thought that she would lose her father's respect. "My big-gest worry was my daddy. What was he going to do? I knew he had to find out about this, but the big question was, 'How?' Eventually, I told my brother. He was very supportive and promised to break the news to my father. In return, he wanted me to promise to have the child. I could not make that promise. I didn't know anything. How could I take care of a baby? I was a baby myself."

Tiffany describes her father, a minister, as a very understanding, sweet man, but when he heard about the pregnancy, the first reac-tion was that he wanted to punch Carter out. He couldn't deal with the fact that his baby was pregnant. Also there was the congrega-tion to consider. Later he admitted that he would have helped to raise the child if Tiffany had wanted it.

"If I had known that, I think I would have kept it," Tiffany says, reflecting. "But he never said a word about it. He couldn't talk to me at all.

"I also worried about the effect on my stepmother, who is very old-fashioned. But she surprised me. She wanted me to make my own decision. She told me, 'Don't depend on that guy. Just depend on yourself.' I was shocked—and relieved."

Although Tiffany could not bring herself to ask her father or Carter for money for an abortion, she was able to ask her uncle. He paid all the medical fees at the clinic where the procedure was performed.

Tiffany describes herself as a religious person who goes to church every Sunday. "I prayed to God about my decision and I think he forgave me."

Jennifer brings Tiffany back to the present predicament with another background question: "Tiffany, what was the first day of your last menstrual period?"

"It was in the second week of January," Tiffany replies, though still absorbed in the earlier abortion.

"And you didn't get one in February?"

"It was very light, very watery." Taking notes on Tiffany's chart, Jennifer continues to ask questions about her menstruation. "Was it on time?"

"It wasn't a normal period."

To determine a pregnancy's duration, it is helpful to have accurate dates. "You got it January 10th and this is March 19th?" the counselor asks.

Tiffany finds it difficult to pay attention to the questions. Her mind races as she prepares for a positive diagnosis. "I don't think I'm going to tell my stepmother this time," she says out loud. "I can't even tell my best friend. I may tell my cousin. Why should I be so upset? I know girls who are much younger than me who have gone through many more pregnancies. I need to get myself together."

Carter is the only person who knows about today's appointment. Before leaving her house, she charged, "I *know I am,* so get your money together."

After her earlier abortion, Carter started coming around again. "He kept apologizing and buying me presents. I don't know how I feel about him. The last time he left me stranded. This time, I'm not paying for anything, not even the doctor bills. Before I was too nervous and I let him get by with too much.

"He's a very fun person and we've had good times together. Right now, I want to do well in school and that's a lot of pressure. Some people can have relationships and do good in school, but that's too much pressure for me. I'm not interested in looking for a man. If he comes, he comes, but I'm not looking."

Jennifer details the urine pregnancy test even though Tiffany had gone through it before. "If the test is positive, have you thought about what you want to do about it?"

"I will terminate it," Tiffany says purposefully. "I'm only eighteen but I feel so old." Tiffany continues to talk while she walks with Jennifer to the examining room. "My mother said that the things that I'm going through as a teenager, she went through long after she was married."

Once inside the examining room, Jennifer gives Tiffany a white drape sheet to put around her. After warm wishes for good luck, Jennifer leaves to greet another client.

Arlene comes in and gives Tiffany the result of the test. Positive. Tiffany smiles at the news, her eyes filling up. "I knew it . . . I knew it. Before I came here I said, 'I know I am . . . I know I am.' But now it's official."

Arlene examines her and learns she is ten to twelve weeks pregnant. This means that Tiffany does not have much time to reach a decision if she is thinking about abortion.

At the post-exam consultation, Arlene begins the discussion with the word "options." Even though Tiffany says she has made up her mind to have an abortion, Arlene has to inform her of the other options available.

Then Arlene moves on to the next topic: contraceptives. Tiffany explains her problems with the pill.

Arlene says, "Usually when a patient experiences nausea, we have her return for a different pill. It is best to take the pill at night, and, to avoid nausea, never on an empty stomach. Talk to us, don't just stop taking it. Maybe you just need a change of pill. There are other means of birth control. Condoms and foam work well but they must be used together to work most effectively. If the condom breaks, you still have the foam which will kill the sperm. Your partner has to be consistent about using the condoms and you have to be consistent about using the foam. It's not, 'This week we'll use the foam . . . this week we'll use the condoms.'

"Birth control takes thought. You can't be carried away by the mood. That should only happen to people in novels. Have you noticed that the women in novels rarely get pregnant? We live in reality. Besides, you have things to do with your life."

Tiffany nods her head.

"Before you start the pills, come back and talk to me about it."

"You won't put me on those bad ones again, not those peach pills?" asks Tiffany.

"Na, we're not that nasty."

Tiffany is about to get up when Arlene gently but firmly takes her arm. There is one more message she wants to pass on to her patient. "Talk to anyone you want to about what to do. But, the final decision is yours. You are the one who has to live with it in your head. Everybody else—including me—offers you options, but you have to make the choice."

Arlene is often disheartened by how rarely teenagers see the correlation between pregnancy and child rearing, or having sex and pregnancy. Another thing that troubles her is that sometimes the decision to maintain or terminate a pregnancy comes from other people: the girl's boyfriend or her family, not the actual patient. Sometimes it is the patient's mother who is thrilled that her daughter is pregnant. One teenager's mother came to every appointment with her. After the birth the mother took care of the baby. The patient complained to Arlene that she didn't feel that the baby was hers. It was her mother's baby. "I had to fight to give my baby a bath. I had to fight to put my baby to bed. To feed my baby. When I tried to talk to my mother about it, she put me down: 'You never know what you're doing.'"

Usually, however, when the mother encourages the teenager to maintain the pregnancy, she is helpful and supportive. Marsha Harper had such a mother.

5

Marsha

MARSHA HARPER didn't go out much. In fact, before her baby was born she had been to only one party. Her evenings were ordinarily spent watching TV and doing homework. When she did go out, it was with her mother, who is divorced, and older twin sisters.

The older girls didn't want their kid sister always to tag along. Her mother thought Marsha was much too young at fifteen to be hanging around with her sisters' boyfriends. In this case, her mother was right because going to the movies with her sisters is exactly how Marsha met the twenty-year-old father of her baby.

Contraceptives were never an issue for Marsha because it never occurred to anyone, least of all Marsha, that she would be having sex. Marsha says, "I was an innocent type. Anyway, I was not interested in sex. I was a tomboy."

Marsha did have an earlier boyfriend, but they never even thought about sex—they thought about having fun. Her second boyfriend, her sister's friend, was older and more pushy. "I thought that I loved him so I said, 'Okay.' I didn't think anything would happen because it was my first time. You'd think you couldn't get pregnant the very first time but I did. I had sex with him once, only once," says Marsha.

For four months Marsha knew that she was pregnant, but was afraid to tell anyone in her close-knit family. Eventually, her mother grew suspicious and called Marsha into the bedroom. Looking her square in the eye, her mother said, "I want to ask you a question. Be truthful. Are you pregnant?"

"No," lied Marsha, turning her head.

"Are you sure?"

"I'm sure."

Her mother persisted until Marsha, crying, broke down and told the truth. She explained that she had heard stories from other kids such as, "If I tell my mother that, she would kill me." That scared Marsha because her mother was her best friend and she didn't want to risk losing her love.

Immediately, they went to Planned Parenthood where Marsha's aunt Brenda happens to be the administrative assistant, and the pregnancy was confirmed.

As far as Marsha was concerned, an abortion was her only solution, but when her sisters were told about the pregnancy, they were supportive and promised to help if she had the child. Marsha wasn't convinced. Her mother voiced the opinion that were she Marsha, she would not have an abortion. Marsha reasoned that the family could not afford another child, but she was told, "We don't have a lot of money but we're making it." With her mother behind her, Marsha felt that having a baby became something to consider.

"I was still so afraid to have it," says Marsha. "Everyone was excited but me." Because she was confused about what to do, she decided the best thing would be to listen to her family. Marsha's boyfriend was thrilled about the pregnancy.

Not everyone was excited. Once the news was out, a number of friends dropped her. She overheard a few of them talking behind her back. Her most painful experience came when the mother of a longtime friend would not allow her daughter to see Marsha for fear that a pregnant teenager would be a bad influence. But her two very best friends stuck by her as did her entire family.

One of the first decisions Marsha did make, though, was to break up with the baby's father. "I did not feel anything for the baby's father anymore. I did not like him. I did not want to be around him. And now I can't stand him."

In school when students stared at her belly, she glowered back. "My stomach was so stretched that I felt that I was going to rip apart. People thought I was carrying twins. It was all water. I never missed a day without eating vanilla ice cream, bananas, and carrot pie. I ate junk food. I ate nutritional food, too, but I did junk food."

Marsha went for a checkup a month before her due date. After the visit to the doctor's office, she planned to go shopping with her mother. In the examining room she was about to get dressed when the doctor returned with a big smile and said, "Do you want to have a baby today?"

Marsha snapped, "No."

He laughed. "Yes, you do."

And she moaned, "Noooooo." He told her to get dressed, make no stops, and go right to the hospital. When a woman is ready to deliver a baby, her cervix opens up about ten centimeters. Marsha's cervix was already seven centimeters wide and had only three more to go.

Mother and daughter flew out of the doctor's office but didn't quite take his advice. Their first stop was at her father's house. Marsha screamed upstairs, "Daddy, hurry up and get dressed, I'm going to have the baby." Their second stop was to pick up her sisters who were on their way to a wedding. They missed the wedding. And then they picked up her aunt, her uncle, her nana. The entire family caravanned to the hospital.

"My mother stayed with me throughout and was my coach. In the last half hour I pushed and pushed and the baby came. A boy, six pounds, three ounces."

Before Marsha became pregnant, she was very thin. She promised herself that she would go on a diet once the baby was born, but she ended up eating more. "Right after I had the baby, my stomach went down and I wasn't big anymore. I felt empty. I missed the stomach. I mentioned that to my doctor, who said it was normal, but I thought I was acting weird."

When Marsha gave birth to Jaret, her mother was thrilled. Here at last was the son she never had. As a young woman, Marsha's mother had adopted twin girls, and had longed for a boy. After Marsha was born, she gave birth to another girl who lived only one day. Because the mother prayed for a boy, she blamed herself for the death. Eventually, after therapy, she felt better.

"My mother stopped seeing her friends in order to spend time with the baby. On her lunch break she would come home and take the baby to work and say, 'This is my son.' She took the baby everywhere. She danced around the house, singing to Jaret." Marsha did not mind her mother's enthusiasm one bit. On the contrary, she was delighted. Marsha says, "Everybody was excited about the baby. He was the most beautiful boy they had ever seen. Everything was great."

Three months after Jaret's birth, Marsha's mother became so ill that she had to leave her job in the middle of the day. Her doctor diagnosed her as having a stomach virus and flu, gave her some medication, and sent her home to rest. The following morning she felt a little better, but as she dressed for work, she became sick again. Marsha's sisters took her to the hospital while Marsha stayed home with the baby. (Usually the sisters took turns baby-sitting because they were both attending college and were able to alternate hours.)

Marsha's mother came home from the hospital that same day feeling better, but by four AM she was running a high fever. Marsha, who always slept with her mother because she had nightmares, says, "That night I noticed rashes all over her face and her body. We called an ambulance. I stayed home with the baby, worrying, while my sisters went to the hospital."

By the time one sister called home, in the wee hours of the morning, most of the family had arrived at the hospital. Her sister told Marsha to dress the baby and come to the hospital immediately. Marsha had expected to hear that everything was fine, that they were coming home, but when she asked how things were going there was a long pause.

"Tell me!" Marsha insisted.

"The doctors are not sure that Mom will live. She has meningitis." Marsha tried to keep herself together. Meanwhile, her aunt and uncle from Manhattan called to say they were on their way and would meet her at the hospital. Once everyone was there, the aunt took care of all the children. Marsha and her uncle went upstairs to see her mother and the doctor. The doctor told the family that if she could make it through the first twenty-four hours, everything would be okay.

Soon her mother was in a coma. She could blink her eyes in response to the family, but she couldn't talk. "She blinked for everyone but me and that made me even more upset. I think that because I was the closest person to her, hearing my voice was agony. The doctors thought so, too. Earlier, in the ambulance, she told my sisters that she was going to die. She kept reaching for them. But she didn't know how to reach for me."

Marsha's mother made it through the first twenty-three hours. Then she suffered a heart attack and died. She was forty-one years old.

Marsha fell apart and had to spend the night at the hospital. For two months she saw a psychiatrist without any easing of the pain she was feeling. She refused to go to school. She would not leave her mother's room. She didn't take care of the baby. She didn't take care of herself.

At age nineteen, Marsha's sisters were too young to become surrogate mothers to Marsha and her baby and they soon moved in with their father. Since he worked from four in the morning to four in the afternoon, he could be of little help with the baby. Marsha says, "I wanted to give up on the baby. I wanted to put him up for adoption." Before long, her aunt, uncle, and their two boys moved in to live with her. The adults slept in the living room because Marsha would not give up her mother's bed.

Finally Marsha reached the point where she was able to feed the baby and change his diapers, but she wouldn't cuddle him or show him love. "That was the thing I should have done, for both of us," she says. "I knew that the baby sensed something was going on. After all, my mother had been with him every second, more than I had been. He wasn't crying, but he wasn't laughing either, and he slept more than usual."

Marsha slowly became stronger. Her uncle, a social worker, taught her how to cope with her grief. He taught her to talk to herself, alone in a room if need be. "I did it," she says. "I talked to myself and cried to myself, and I got better each day. I got to the point where I could put my mother's clothes into storage."

Eventually she asked her uncle and aunt to move into the master bedroom. They were surprised and delighted because they could see that Marsha was becoming herself again. "Then we started cleaning the house. We disinfected everything. In one day I cleaned her room. I did the living room. We switched the furniture all around. We did a lot of shopping and redecorating. Now we are all comfortable and living together.

"My baby's father wants to have a relationship with me again. He tells me that we could be happy together, be a family. I'm not ready for that. He takes his responsibility seriously. He helps financially and visits regularly. But we're not close. There's something about him . . . I don't like being around him much."

Marsha's day begins at seven o'clock. Before waking the baby, she dresses for school. While she bathes and dresses Jaret, her aunt takes care of her own two kids. Breakfast is no longer prepared at home. Marsha and her aunt drive the kids to the baby-sitter for breakfast. After school she takes some time for herself watching TV or napping. When her aunt returns from work, they pick up their

Marsha and Jaret, with a picture of Marsha's mother

children. All three kids play with Marsha while her aunt and uncle prepare dinner. Marsha taught her nephews, two- and four-year-olds, to ride their bikes. Jaret doesn't do much yet. He stands and walks while holding onto furniture. Outside he plays in the walker. The only thing he says is "Da Da." "He claps, bites his toes, and does silly things," says Marsha. "He'll start laughing for no reason. Weird child. At dinnertime I feed him first and put him to bed."

Jaret usually wakes up in the evening around nine and Marsha holds him. Then, in the quiet of the evening, she looks at her baby and thinks of her mother. "He looks just like her," she says. Her aunt and uncle often sing Jaret back to sleep. Music fills the Harper household once again.

Marsha's girlfriends tell her that when they watch her with her baby, they dream about having one of their own, as cute as Jaret, to love and to cuddle. Marsha tells them, "There is a big difference between watching someone else's kid play and having your own. I worked as an assistant at a day-care center for two years and it was easy. I got to leave the kids at six o'clock and go home. Having my own baby is a whole different ball game. I can't say, 'I don't feel like watching him now.'"

Marsha easily becomes irritated by Jaret's constant need for attention. "I actually say, 'I don't feel like being bothered, somebody take the baby.' If no one is around to do it, I make the baby sit down and he'll scream and cry. I'll just ignore him." Marsha's aunt and uncle have told her to give them the baby to care for when she is feeling like that. If she does, she feels bad because that's her responsibility. She admits, "I'm still very childish. I like to act silly with my friends. I like to do what other seventeen-year-olds do: shop, talk on the phone, play in the park."

Until she is eighteen Marsha will receive her mother's social security check every month. With it she buys the baby's food and necessities. Whatever money is left goes into the bank. She shares the expenses for the baby-sitter with the baby's father. "So I'm making it," says Marsha, "but it is nothing like playing house."

Only very recently has Marsha been able to talk about her mother. She still becomes depressed on certain occasions, such as last Christmas when a number of her relatives were at her house.

The other day Marsha's aunt's mother visited from the South. "My baby's mother, me, was there. My two cousins' mother was there. Even my aunt's mother was there. Everybody's mother was there except mine. It was especially hard that day."

6

"Am I an Insensitive Person?"

TWO teary-eyed sophomores, Annie (name and identity changed) and Louise (name and identity changed) are anxious about having had abortions. Annie, a short, skinny, sixteen-year-old, appears unsure of herself. One night, while sleeping, she sat up in her bed and saw MURDERER written on her bedroom wall in blood. She awoke screaming.

Ultra-sophisticated Louise is in tears, too, but for a different reason. After her abortion she felt nothing other than relief. She thought that her decision was the only way to go. Once done, she put it behind her and apparently never gave it a second thought. "Am I an insensitive person?" she asks while winding long strands of her lush, red hair around artfully colored fingers.

Annie and Louise choose to go together to see Maxine, the counselor at Planned Parenthood. During their interview Annie tells Maxine that she would have liked to keep the baby. "I'm not interested in continuing my education. I don't have a burning desire for some fancy career. The rest of my life doesn't look too great. Perhaps a baby, my very own baby, to love and play with, would make it better. My mother had different ideas. Even though we are Catholic, she insisted that I have an abortion. If we had told my father about it, he would have gone berserk."

Maxine asks her what she would have done if the choice was her own. She shrugs her shoulders and says, "I guess I would have had the kid and asked somebody like you about a home or something."

Louise sits listening as her friend speaks. Turning pale, she squirms in her chair. When it is her turn to speak, she begins by talking about the day of the abortion. She went into the doctor's office while a friend waited outside to drive her home. Neither she nor her boyfriend wanted a baby. This seemingly self-assured young woman knew what she wanted to do with her life and a baby would be in the way. She is mainly upset that her boyfriend, who paid the entire bill, did not offer to come with her. They broke up soon after the procedure.

"Why did you want to see me?" Maxine asks her.

"I'm worried about my reaction, or my nonreaction. Why am I so casual about it? Am I an insensitive person? Am I self-centered?" She begins to cry.

After an abortion the woman is typically so relieved that it's over that she doesn't want to be reminded of it. But there are exceptions. Some of these exceptions return to Planned Parenthood to help sort out their feelings. Maxine works with the clients who have had trouble coming to terms with their decisions. She encourages them to go through a mourning period, similar to the way they would mourn a miscarriage. "Just because the pregnancy ended voluntarily doesn't mean the woman can't mourn that decision. If she tries to bury her feelings, they may pop up, sometimes when least expected."

Maxine helps her clients come to terms with the past and then prepare for the future. The future, as far as Maxine is concerned, means birth control. "Our experience has been that it is unrealistic to expect that a person who has been sexually active will suddenly stop. She won't go back into celibacy. Therefore, she must learn how to protect herself. She can't go through this again and again."

7

"Back to My Normal Self"

Roxanne, 18 (Name and identity changed)

"WAIT-wait-wait," says Roxanne, a slim, bouncy young woman in a khaki jumpsuit and red leather cowboy boots. "Let me take my boots off, they add to my weight." She slips off her boots, kicks them to the corner, and steps onto the scale. "Wait-wait-wait again, let me take my bracelets off, and my rings."

Jennifer Wilson laughs. "Why not take everything off. You're so skinny anyway. . . ." They giggle together, talking like friends who have known each other for a long time. Yet they only met when Roxanne became pregnant.

Now, two weeks after the termination of her pregnancy, Roxanne is seeing Jennifer at the clinic for a checkup and birth control pills.

Roxanne has been sexually active since she was sixteen. She and Steve (name and identity changed), eighteen, her boyfriend of two years, were relying on the withdrawal method as a means of contraception. She says, "Some people say this method is fine, but it's not, because a little bit of sperm can trickle out to get you pregnant. That's what happened with me.

"I had serious thoughts of keeping the child. Lying in bed late at night I thought, 'I know that I'm pregnant! I can't believe this is happening.' I was confused. I wondered, 'If I have an abortion, am I killing my child? Will the embryo feel pain? Will it understand? I hope I'm not three months pregnant, I hope I'm only a week pregnant.'"

When Roxanne confided to Steve that she was pretty sure she was pregnant, his response was simple. "You have to see a doctor and get this taken care of as soon as possible."

"But wait a second," Roxanne replied. "You don't understand, I may want to go through with this." Steve was devastated. Every night he went out to get drunk, get stoned, get as far away from "the accident" as drugs and booze could take him. He would promise to see her, but then he wouldn't show up. Roxanne says, "He was gone! I was a total wreck. The only thing I was able to do was cry, every day, every night."

The second person Roxanne confided in was her older sister, who responded, "I'm behind you 100 percent, whatever you choose to do. If you want to have a child, I'll be there for you. We can work it out some way. But I want you to realize something. You're eighteen. You're in love with your body. You do modeling. You have a great job. You make good money. You don't need a man to take care of you. Once you have a child, you can't go out on the weekends like you did before. You'll be restricted in a lot of the things you love to do."

Roxanne's third confidant was her mother, who became increasingly unnerved as she heard about the problem. "Of course it upsets me to know that my little Roxanne is having sex, but if you are, I want you to be protected from pregnancy or disease. How could you have let this happen?" she asked. "I've told you so many things . . . I told you to go on the pill . . . Why? . . . Why? . . . Why? . . . I'm shocked . . . THIS NEVER HAPPENED TO YOUR SISTER!"

Eventually her mother pulled herself together and said they

would go to Planned Parenthood to find the best place for an abortion.

When Roxanne said that she wanted to have the child, her mother's reaction was similar to Steve's, although she did not turn to drink and drugs. "She said I would ruin my life. I would have to leave home. My boyfriend would abandon me. I began having second thoughts. I did not want to bring a child into this world if I didn't even have my own mother behind me."

For two weeks everything was centered around Roxanne's pregnancy. When her father was first told about it, he couldn't talk to her. "He couldn't face me. My father's a quiet man. He couldn't look me in the eyes and say, 'Listen, I don't want you to have a child,' which is exactly what I wanted to hear him say. Instead, without a word to me from my father, my mother said, 'And your father agrees with me 100 percent.'"

Roxanne asked, "Dad, do you agree with her?"

Painfully he replied, "Yeah, I do. But I'm here for you, whatever you decide." Somehow that made Roxanne feel a lot better.

Roxanne began experiencing emotions she never felt before. Her breasts were swelling and she was becoming very irritable. "I was screaming, yelling, freaking out. My sister would kid around with me, and I'd scream at her to leave me alone."

Steve expected Roxanne not to be upset, not to be emotional. She should get the abortion, and that's it. He admitted that he was sad about what they had to do, but he was just not ready to become a father. When he confided his dilemma to his own father the reaction was, "What's wrong with you? Are you stupid? You should have used something." But then he came around and promised to give Steve money for the abortion.

Roxanne became more demanding of Steve. "If you don't come over, I'm having this child."

He fired back, "It probably isn't even mine."

Roxanne was seething. "You know damn well I've never slept with anyone else. I took criminal justice, HONEY, I know that child is yours and I'll have blood tests to prove it. You will pay for this." She felt utterly abandoned by him.

Steve, on the other hand, says he simply couldn't handle the shock that his girlfriend was pregnant. Finally, he went to her house one night and apologized for his behavior. The whole mess was hard for him to accept. He couldn't understand why she would want to have a child at this time in their lives. The important thing for Steve was that they stay together.

Roxanne was most upset about how nonchalant Steve was, expecting her to simply "get on with it."

"You're right," he confessed. "I don't understand. I'm not a woman, and I never will understand."

"I wish you could be the one going through this," Roxanne cried softly. "You would be the one worrying."

Once Steve learned that Roxanne would go through with an abortion, he acted differently and was more loving, more caring. "That upset me in a way," she says.

Roxanne decided to go to Planned Parenthood for a pregnancy test rather than to her family doctor because two of her girlfriends had gone there and liked the way they were treated.

Once in the counseling session with Jennifer, she said, "I can put down a million dollars that I know I'm pregnant." Jennifer agreed that everything she told her indicated that she might be pregnant. The test, as suspected, came back positive.

After her physical exam, Arlene Mayo, the nurse practitioner, diagnosed her pregnancy as between six and eight weeks. That's what Roxanne had figured.

Roxanne says, "Once the nurse confirmed it, I went into shock. Now my assumptions were a fact, and you can't beat a real fact. I ran out crying."

By that time Roxanne had decided that she would definitely go for an abortion. The bottom line was that she did not want to bring into the world a child that did not have a father or grandparents who wanted it.

She went home and told her parents that her pregnancy was official. Roxanne's mother was reassuring and said that they would go through this together. Resolute, she called one of the doctor's offices from the list that Arlene had given her.

Roxanne questioned all her friends who had had abortions. She says, "I was concerned about the elasticity of my vagina. I wanted to keep myself nice and tight. I have this thing about being clean and being tight." She was also very concerned about how she would feel afterward. Was she going to have bad cramps? Would she be sick? She asked her best friend, "A few weeks later, did it still shock you or did you just forget about it?" Her friend replied, "Believe it or not, just having that worry over and done with made me feel so much better."

The week before the abortion, Steve finally became supportive. Roxanne says, "I think the only reason I said I was having the child was to spite him. He was totally ignoring me that first week."

The night before the abortion Roxanne was so distraught she became sick. She couldn't even keep ginger ale down. It got to the point where she was throwing up yellow bile. The clinic had told her not to eat anything after midnight, but that didn't matter, she had no interest in food. When it got to the point where she was throwing up green intestinal juices, her skin began flaking because she was so dehydrated.

The morning of the procedure finally came. Steve and her sister went with her to the clinic. "My boyfriend became very emotional, but remained supportive. He kept hugging me and saying I was going to be all right." Roxanne threw up in the car. "My appointment was at nine, but we arrived at eight-forty-seven. I remember it exactly. I was really nervous. The clinic was just packed with women between the ages of fifteen and twenty-four. Some were freaked out, some fine, and some were sitting there with glazed looks on their faces, the same look as mine. The I-don't-believe-this-is-happening look. I tried to keep a good attitude, because I was told that I would feel better when I awoke. I tried, did I ever try."

When the receptionist told Roxanne to be seated, Steve and her sister went outside to wait for her. Roxanne explained that she had been extremely sick with morning sickness. She was ushered into the recovery room to relax because no one was there yet. "There were nice, neat, clean, very clean beds lined up against the walls. I threw up again, then lay down on one of the beds.

"Once I was feeling a little better, I returned to the waiting room and talked to the other women. Some of them were there for a second or third time and I wondered how these women could let this happen. One girl had become pregnant only a month after she had had an abortion. She started to have sex before she started having normal periods again. She thought that she didn't need protection until she got her period. She was wrong. You can become pregnant again. After I heard that I thought, 'I will make sure.' We shared our feelings about morning sickness, anxieties, and reasons for having an abortion. It was like group therapy. That time with the other women was soothing.

"A nurse took me to a dressing room and said, 'Take off all your clothes and put the gown on facing back.' That's when I REALLY got upset and started crying. I hoped God would forgive me for what I was doing. I prayed that the baby would understand. I promised that when I'm all done having children and I don't want to have another one, I'll have one more anyway just to make myself suffer for what I did when I was eighteen. That was my promise to God.

"My nurse saw that I was a wreck and she was so cool. I just loved this lady. I thanked God she was there. She kept saying, 'Calm down, calm down.' She made me feel so much better.

"Once inside the operating room, there were two male doctors, a few female nurses, and a woman anesthetist. Because my blood pressure was low, the anesthetist couldn't find a vein and asked another doctor to take over. I guess he was more experienced with the 'no vein, skinny people.'

"The doctor was really nice. I said to him, 'Please, Doctor, be gentle.'

"He smiled. 'I'm always gentle.'

"'Please wait till I'm out.'

"'We're going to wait till you're out.'

"Their friendliness made me calm down a bit. Then the doctor gave me a physical exam just to be sure I was pregnant. 'I can guarantee that it's eight weeks,' I said.

"'Feels like it to me,' he replied.

"They put in the intravenous and within five seconds I was out. When I first woke up I cried because I felt stomach cramps. Two fifteen-year-old girls were there already eating cookies and drinking ginger ale. These girls were younger than me! I couldn't believe how cool they were. But there were two other girls who were screaming at the top of their lungs, 'I don't believe I did this,' and the nurses were trying to calm them down. Those nurses were busy. They were back and forth, helping everybody.

"I cried, 'I'm in pain, I'm in pain.' And my nurse said, 'I know you're in pain, but keep saying, "It's over."'

"I started saying, 'It's over . . . it's over . . . it's over . . .' The cramping let up a little and I began feeling better. I still felt nauseous, but that was from the anesthesia, not the pregnancy."

Soon Roxanne dressed and went outside where her sister and Steve had been waiting. Their first question was, "How do you feel?"

"I feel all right. I feel better. I want to go home." They had bought her a teddy bear and a big balloon, which made her smile. After all this, they couldn't believe how in control she was.

Once home, the nausea completely stopped. Roxanne had cramps that felt like her normal period. Steve made her a hot water bottle, brought ginger ale, and played with her hair. "I'm here. I'm here," he said. Roxanne's mother, who was at work, called every five minutes. Eventually both Roxanne and Steve fell asleep in her room.

Three hours later she awoke, feeling great, and dying for a roast beef sandwich. Steve raced to a nearby deli and bought the sandwich and french fries.

Her mother returned home to find her daughter sitting up in bed, eating. "Oh, thank God," her mother exclaimed. When Roxanne began making smarty remarks, her mother laughed. "I can tell you're better already. You're being a smart mouth." Then she began crying.

By the next day the bleeding had stopped and Roxanne felt great. Within a few days she began working out, going to the steam room, tanning. She and her boyfriend were back to normal and she was no longer irritable.

Two weeks later

Two weeks have since passed and it is safe for Roxanne to resume sexual relations. She insists that Steve wear a condom, "just to be doubly sure." Roxanne chose to return to Planned Parenthood for her post-abortion checkup even though she could have had a free checkup at the doctor's office where she had the abortion. Roxanne felt that she never wanted to see that place again, even though she was very well treated.

Arlene Mayo tells her that her uterus is back to normal and there are no complications. Following a lengthy discussion about contraceptives, Arlene, smiling, says, "Go back to your life."

"When Steve and I were fighting about the pregnancy, I thought, 'Yeah, you think you're going to touch me again.' I was sure that this experience might turn me off sex forever. It didn't. We are stronger and even more devoted to one another. I feel the way I used to feel about him. I thought I was going to feel very guilty afterwards, but I don't. Now, I'm back to my normal self."

8

"Will It Hurt?"

New Jersey

THE waiting room inside the red-brick building housing the Metropolitan Associates, Inc. is crowded. This clinic is licensed by the state of New Jersey to terminate a pregnancy up to twenty-one weeks. (With rare exceptions abortions cannot be done after twenty-four weeks.) It also does free pregnancy tests and has a referral service should a woman want to continue her pregnancy. For the most part, though, when a woman comes here she knows that she is pregnant and has decided to have an abortion.

On the second floor, the nonmedical floor, a line of people waiting to check in snakes around the aisles of beige cushioned seats and out toward the top of the stairs. Telephones ring endlessly. Saturday morning is the busiest day at the clinic. Nancy Buckley, an attractive women, thirty-something, who doubles as a receptionist and a doctor's assistant, energetically checks off patients' names, answers questions, and hands out mimeographed forms. A teenage couple wearing matching jeans and sweatshirts and sporting indistinguishable haircuts stand before her, first in line.

Nancy tries, in vain, to address questions and instructions to the girl, but her male companion does all the talking. The patients are called only by their first name and last initial to insure anonymity.

"My girlfriend's name is Tracy L (name and identity changed). How long is this going to take? Will it hurt?" Nancy answers him and deliberately hands the medical form to Tracy. The couple choose seats in the center of the room. The boy dictates her medical information while she writes. Once all the questions are answered, Tracy returns the sheet to Nancy. Then, in an attempt to detach themselves from what is about to happen, they watch a video on the TV monitor located on the wall in the middle of the room.

"Tracy L," a lab technician eventually calls the patient. Tracy kisses her boyfriend good-bye and follows the nurse to the lab for a pregnancy test to confirm the diagnosis as well as various blood tests. Then she returns to the waiting room until her name is called again for a counseling session. No one has an abortion without a counseling session.

In the middle of the room, a tall, well-dressed girl sits all bunched up in a long, red coat. Next to her, erect and reserved, is her mother. Neither speaks.

"Letty W (name and identity changed)," the nurse calls at the door. Still clinging to her coat, the girl stands, as does her mother.

Letty W, 17

Throughout the counseling session, Letty is unable to look at the social worker, Randi Fortgang, or her mother. Instead, she clutches her coat like a security blanket.

Randi begins the session with a question. "Have you ever been pregnant before?"

"No," Letty replies.

"Have you been using any kind of birth control in the past?"

"No." Letty is painfully shy, her answers practically inaudible.

Randi writes Letty's responses onto the medical chart. Then she counsels Letty about alternatives to abortion. If Randi sensed that Letty was not sure about her decision, she would discuss options in greater detail. Letty appears certain about her choice.

Then, in minute detail, the counselor describes the procedure that Letty will undergo. "Basically, after you leave this room, you will return to the waiting room and have a seat. The next time your name is called, you will pay your fee and go downstairs. A nurse will bring you into a dressing room and give you a cotton gown to put on. You can wear your jewelry and socks, but nothing else. After you are in your gown, she will accompany you to the operating room. There they will put an IV, intravenous, into a vein in your arm for anesthesia. We have two kinds of anesthesia that are given intravenously. One kind, general anesthesia, puts you to sleep. Every patient's history is reviewed before becoming a candidate for general. For example, if you weighed over two hundred pounds we would not give a general. That is not a problem for you. The second kind is a local. That is, we give a mixture of valium and demerol to dull the pain. It will make you relax and feel somewhat out of it. Then, we numb the cervix with a novocaine paracervical block. In this procedure you will be awake. Which would you prefer?"

"I want to sleep," Letty says firmly.

"Okay," replies Randi, "according to your medical history there should be no problem, so long as you haven't had anything to eat or drink since midnight." A person going under anesthesia cannot have anything to eat or drink after midnight. Doctors are very strict about that because when an IV containing sodium brevatol begins to drip, a patient loses her gag reflex. Whatever is in the stomach will come up. One of the biggest hazards with anesthesia is the possibility of aspiration, when a patient vomits while on the operating table and inhales her disgorge into her lungs.

"I haven't eaten." Letty returns to whispers. During Randi's narration, no communication passes between the mother and the daughter. The mother appears to be on another planet—anywhere but here. She stares at an unadorned beige wall, rocking slowly from side to side.

Randi continues to instruct her patient. "You're early on in the pregnancy; therefore, the kind of procedure we will perform is called a D & C. After the IV is inserted, the doctor will come in, introduce himself, review your medical chart, and ask you when you had your last period. He will also ask if you've had anything to eat or drink. We all ask that question. Then the doctor will examine you to determine the length of the pregnancy. Once done, medication goes into the IV and you fall asleep.

"Because at this stage in the pregnancy the cervix is too small to allow the removal of tissue, the doctor needs to widen, or dilate, it. To do that, he will use a series of progressively wider instruments called dilators. After the dilation of the cervix, a curette is inserted which scrapes the uterine walls to loosen the pregnancy. Then another instrument, called a vacurette, will be inserted through your dilated cervix, and continue up into your uterus. The vacurette acts as a suction tube and removes the contents of the uterus. Then the doctor uses the curette again to make sure all tissue is removed. The whole procedure takes about three to five minutes. The next thing you know, you will wake up in the recovery room, and it will all be over."

Throughout Randi's description, Letty seems to be in a stupor. "Do you understand all this?" the counselor asks out loud.

No reply.

"Do you have any questions?"

No questions.

Randi isn't finished. "Once you are home, have something to eat and then rest. You'll be fine, but take it easy today. To prevent infection we're going to give you antibiotics to begin taking after you've eaten. We will also give you another medication to control bleeding and help to contract the uterus. The bleeding is like a period or lighter. Some people only bleed for a few days while for others it could be about a week. If you experience very heavy bleeding or you pass lots of clots of blood, you should call us right away.

"You might feel cramps today. If you do, take a nonaspirin pain control, like Tylenol. Aspirin might make you bleed more. And, for the next two weeks, we don't want you to have sex . . ."

Letty's eyes widen as her mother's narrow. "That's okay," Letty says softly, implying that sex is the last thing on her mind at present.

". . . or douche, swim, or take a tub bath. You can shower. At the end of that two-week period you must go for a checkup. You wrote in your chart that you will go to your mother's doctor afterwards. He should be able to supply you with birth control."

Letty's mother, brought back to earth by the word "sex," begins to participate in the discussion. "My doctor told us about that," she tells Randi.

The counseling continues. "You should get your normal period in about four to six weeks. We ask that every patient sign this standard consent form." The form states how many weeks pregnant Letty is and it describes the complications that can occur. The counselor explains these complications, too. Each patient must read the form before signing and the counselor must make sure that she understands what she is signing.

After Letty signs her form, Randi asks if she has any questions. She does not, but her mother interjects, "I'm sick about this."

Randi nods, acknowledging the mother's sorrow, but her primary concern is Letty. "Do you have any questions?"

"I just want to know if it is going to hurt," Letty murmurs.

"No." Randi smiles sympathetically. "You're going to be totally asleep. When you awake, you'll ask, 'How come I haven't been taken yet?'" Letty's fingers finally lessen their grip on the coat.

"And I'm going to be happy to get this over with," her mother adds, adjusting her hat.

The petite Randi stands beside Letty who towers over her. She wants to repeat an important piece of information. "In the next couple of weeks, if you experience anything unusual, for example, very heavy bleeding, a fever, or bad cramping, call us. I don't care if it's in the middle of the night. Never, ever delay."

Letty begins to waver as she stands up to leave. Her mother steadies her daughter and they embrace. For a moment or two, the mother holds her daughter protectively, while stroking her hair.

9

"Please Say It's the Flu"

IN THE second-floor staff lounge a pot of coffee perks beside a large round table that is covered with danish, bagels, and Greek pastry. Earlier, Nicholas Poulos, one of the clinic's three gynecologists, stopped by his favorite bakery to bring the staff these goodies. The staff needs the lounge to help them unwind. Randi takes a short break between patients and munches a pastry while peeking through the curtains to the street outside. An anti-abortion demonstration across the street is becoming shrill. They beg, plead, and scream for patients not to enter the clinic.

"There's a young girl getting out of a car and the right-to-lifers are harassing her. They're trying to show her pictures. It's making me sick," she tells the others in the room.

Another aide joins her. "Look at it, it's disgusting. There's a man shoving pictures of bloody babies at that young girl."

"Is he allowed to do that?" a third staff member asks.

Susan Martinelli, the director of the clinic, refuses to look out the window. "He is allowed, if he stays across the street," she says. Eventually, unable to resist, Susan peeks through the side of the venetian blind. "That client couple should not have parked their car over there," she says irritably. "Now she has to get out on the demonstrators' side." Susan, whose youthful appearance belies her position, tries to sustain a detached, professional air. Generally she succeeds, but the tilt of her head, a wry smile, or warm, laughing eyes often betray her posture. By now, Susan is glued to the window. "Mike is on the job. He will take care of it," she says, as she watches the burly security guard go to the couple's rescue.

Margot B, 16 (Name and identity changed)

Mike escorts the rescued couple and their companions upstairs. Margot signs in as the others find four empty seats in the center aisle. Margot, a buxom brunette, casually dressed in a navy blue running suit and white sneakers, sits on her boyfriend's lap. His name is Vic (name and identity changed). Seated protectively around the couple are Margot's sister, her sister's fiancé, and Margot's best friend. They are stone-faced, all except Margot, who is madly in love. Unashamedly, she hugs and kisses Vic, practically oblivious to the others in the room. Vic holds his girlfriend tightly, almost catatonic, unable to move a muscle.

After her counseling session with Susan, Margot talks about Vic and her decision. "My Vic is big with muscles all over the place." But Vic is more than just a great body. "He's my big, tender bear. If I get a scratch, he says, 'Oh, let me kiss your boo-boo.'"

Margot says, "This mistake is all my fault. I didn't tell my doctor that I was on the pill when he prescribed an antibiotic to ward off a kidney infection." Broad spectrum antibiotics diminish the potency of low-dose birth control pills. Margot did not know that at the time. "That's why it's important to report that you're on the pill if a doctor asks if you are taking any medication," Margot adds.

Margot waited twenty weeks, nearly the cutoff period at this clinic, before she was able to pull together all the pieces necessary for her to have an abortion. Why so long?

"First of all, I wanted to know all my options. Making this decision was even more scary than having sex for the first time. That took long enough as it was. Secondly, whatever I decided to do about the pregnancy, I needed money, lots of money. I didn't have any.

"Vic and I have been together for over a year and we plan to be married. He was my first. And, as far as I know, I was his, too. When I missed a period, I thought, 'Oh, my God, I've got to get this checked out.'

"Planned Parenthood confirmed my worst nightmares. I was positive. I panicked. The main thought that raced through my mind was, 'He's not ready for this, he's going to leave me.'"

After leaving Planned Parenthood, Margot went straight to Vic's. Vic answered the doorbell to find Margot standing there, downcast. "It's the flu . . . it's the flu . . . please say it's the flu," he pleaded.

Holding up the slip of paper with the results of the pregnancy test, she whispered, "I'm sorry." His mouth dropped open.

Margot reacted to Vic's stunned expression by switching gears. "If you're scared, you can walk. I'll be upset, but I'm not going to make you stay with me."

That was never an issue for Vic. As far as he was concerned, the pregnancy was half his responsibility. "The pregnancy came from love and the decision should be made with love," he said.

"Vic's conclusion was simple: abortion. He said, 'We're too young to have children. We should go to college and make something of ourselves.' He promised me that in the future we would have children.

"Even though I agreed with his reasoning, I wasn't entirely sure of what I wanted. I thought, 'I'm close to graduation and I have a part-time job. If I really tried, I could go through with this and have the baby.' Then I changed my mind: 'If I were to have a child, and Vic left me, I'd be stuck with something I'm really not ready for.' The only thing that I was sure about was that the final decision was going to be mine. Vic agreed.

"Night and day, the 'big D' was all I could think about. Was I being realistic? Was I being selfish? I needed time. Finally, I came to the conclusion that Vic was right, motherhood was unimaginable at this time.

"Before I became pregnant, Vic and I went out all the time. Now, all I wanted to do was sleep. We were still having sex. Why not? I wouldn't get pregnant. But for the last two weeks he hasn't wanted to."

Margot has an open and realistic relationship with her parents. In fact, she confided in her mother when she decided to become sexually active. "I told my mother when I was ready to have sex," Margot says. Her mother, who is pragmatic about her children, cautioned her to be careful. "Telling them about sex was one thing. Telling them about my pregnancy is quite another story. I thought that they would be disappointed in me. After all, how could such a smart girl like me do such a dumb thing like that? I didn't want to disillusion them. The only person in my family I could confide in was my older sister."

"'Tell Mom,' my sister urged.

"'No, I must take care of this myself.'"

By this time, Margot was beginning her second trimester. This particular New York clinic where she went for a procedure was not licensed to do second trimester abortions. There was no other choice but to *tell Mom*.

"I told my family while we sat around the kitchen table. 'I have something awful to tell you. I'm pregnant.' I was pretty emotional. I couldn't look my parents in the eyes. They, on the other hand, just sat there staring straight at me in disbelief. My sister had been born when our mother was sixteen. She had told us stories about how difficult it was for her to have a baby at that age, my age. Though my mother loves my sister, she felt that life cheated her. Now she faced me, her daughter, stuck with the same problem. She was very comforting about it.

"The absolute worst part was telling my father. This would be the first time in my life that I disappointed him and I dreaded his reaction. That was wrong, too. My father was furious at me for not coming to them sooner. I must admit that telling my family was a big relief."

Margot did not want to ask her parents for money unless absolutely necessary, but it was necessary. Though they are not wealthy, they were able to come up with most of the fee. Vic's mother paid the balance even though she would have preferred that Margot give her a grandchild.

Once all the decisions were in place, Vic felt better. Until today, the actual day of the procedure.

Margot's sister picked everyone up and drove them to the clinic. In the backseat of the car, Margot put her head in Vic's lap and fell asleep. He rested his head on top of hers and also fell asleep. As they drove up the street toward the clinic, Margot's sister noticed the large crowd of anti-abortion pickets. She awakened the couple. "I'm just warning you there is a mess outside. Don't let them get to you, they are just ignorant." Margot said that she could handle it. She says, "I can understand how the people feel out there, but I wish that they would understand how we feel in here."

Mike ushered the group past the bellowing crowd and safely inside, they silently watched a video, *Big,* being shown in the waiting room.

Margot says, "I'm not really scared. I know this is a good place. I was nervous on the way up. My last meal was at seven o'clock last night and now, ten AM, I'm starved."

Forty-five minutes later, Margot's name is called. She kisses each of her companions good-bye and walks through the door for the preparatory part of the procedure.

Margot goes into Susan's office for a counseling session. Susan explains everything that is about to happen. Patients in their second trimester (thirteen to twenty-eight weeks) are examined by a gynecologist on the second floor in order to determine the proper procedure. An internal examination is followed by a sonogram, an ultrasound picture of the uterus, to determine the duration of the pregnancy. The fetus at this stage of development is too large to go through the undilated cervix. An abortion could tear the cervix.

The procedure that Margot will undergo is called a late D & E, that is Dilation and Evacuation. In this clinic patients who are pregnant over sixteen weeks must first have a laminaria insertion. (Some doctors do it earlier.) That involves a seaweed-like "tampon" implanted into the cervix to help dilate it. The moisture from the cervix makes the laminaria expand, which causes the cervix to gradually dilate. After this procedure the patient must wait approximately three hours. During this period, she cannot eat, drink, or smoke because she will be undergoing anesthesia later. (This procedure varies greatly. For example, at Metropolitan patients over twenty-one weeks must wait overnight or even longer.)

After the counseling session, Margot pays her fee. Then she is examined by Dr. Poulos. He reads her medical record and does a sonogram. When he inserts the laminaria, he explains in advance everything that he will be doing as well as what his patient will be feeling.

Afterward she says, "I'm okay about this. The only thing I'm not okay about is the people outside the building. I don't think that they have any right to tell me what I can or cannot do with my body." She focuses her uneasiness on the anonymous group, chanting across the street.

"I want to be a musician. I play the guitar. Vic is going to be a football coach, like his father. I get better grades than he does. He's very bright, but you wouldn't know it by looking at him. He just sits there and vegetates, but I love him," Margot says affectionately.

10

"It's Hard to Be a Teenager Now"

ON THE following Saturday, 9:30 AM, two protest groups are marching and shouting across the street from the Metropolitan clinic. The group on the right side of the street carry graphic posters. One is shaped like a tombstone with blood red lettering announcing, "Your Baby!"

The group on the left side of the street carry pro-choice placards. A preppie-looking man carries a sign that reads, "Honk if you are pro-choice." Many "honking" cars drive by. Each group stick to their designated turf and shout angrily at the other.

Around the corner, in a phone booth, a woman calls the clinic, afraid to keep her appointment because of the picketers. Nancy arranges for Mike, the security guard, to escort her and shield her from the mob.

People have looked through the garbage bins of Metropolitan clinic, thinking they will find dead babies. There was even a story in a local newspaper reporting that a baby was found which was traceable to the clinic. "That is absolute nonsense," says Dr. Poulos. "For one, the tissue does not come out as a whole fetus. Besides, all the products of conception are sent to a laboratory for a pathology report."

Demonstrators outside the Metropolitan clinic

The waiting room is filling up fast. A good-looking twenty-nine-year-old blond man sits on the top step, outside the waiting room, with his eight-year-old son. They share an apple while they wait for their wife and mother to come out of anesthesia.

Inside, Nancy explains the clinic's price structure to a high school freshman who says she is nineteen weeks pregnant. The girls and their boyfriends are easily spotted by their ashen look, while the faces of their accompanying friends and family are flushed with trying to ease the tension. A young couple approach Nancy. The boy says, "My girlfriend is here for an abortion. She is twenty-one weeks pregnant. Is there any risk?"

"There is always a risk with surgery, but we have three excellent doctors who do this procedure every day. I'll have the counselor talk to you about it."

Already in the waiting room, two teenage girls and a boy sit in the corner. The girls, a blonde and a brunette, have permed hair and wear designer jeans and oversize T-shirts whose elaborate logo announces the latest heavy metal concert. The blonde sits on the boy's lap. All are giggling. After a while the blonde's name is called for her procedure. The once-assured boy looks up—his eyes fill with tears as his girlfriend hesitantly goes inside.

Meanwhile, two other girls, both nineteen, enter the room and approach the front desk. They are dressed in exactly the same outfits. It turns out they are the same age, they come from the same town, and they have had the same menstrual period dates. Both take pregnancy tests that are positive.

"We're keeping it," they shout at the exact same time, and bound out of the office, leaving the staff speechless.

Lisa M, 17 (Name and identity changed)

All alone in the waiting room, as far away from the video as possible, seventeen-year-old Lisa has been watching the antics of the two teenage look-alikes. Lisa did not fully understand that the clinic will not give her general anesthesia unless someone is here to drive her home. Like everyone else about to have an abortion, she hasn't had anything to eat since midnight. The lack of food has brought on a terrible headache.

"I have too many things to do before becoming a mother. I must graduate high school and then go on to the college where I won a tennis scholarship. I don't need emotional support. What I do need is to get this over with and go on with my life."

Lisa gives the impression of a young woman in total control of her life. It's not what she says, necessarily, but the style and body language she uses when she says it. "As far as I can tell, there is no reason to tell anyone about the procedure other than my boyfriend and best girlfriend. I know what the problem is and I'm having it fixed. I've taken care of all the details. That's it." All but one, as it turns out.

Suddenly, Lisa's mood shifts and the little girl in her materializes. "Oh, God! I feel so sick. I really don't feel well." She quickly collects herself. "Although my boyfriend is sympathetic, I didn't want him to be here with me. I once told him, 'If I become pregnant, I don't think I will tell you. I want to get it over with by myself.' He said he felt left out and somewhat offended by my comment. My girlfriend will be here in a few hours to take me home.

"Once fiction became fact, I was more emotional than I expected. It took me a long time to finally admit to my boyfriend that I thought I was pregnant. When I did, he said, 'Everything will be okay. I'll help you in every way.' And that was that. There was no other discussion, no choices to consider.

"We're pretty rational when it comes to things like this. We're both too young to have a child. A conflict arises when one person wants to keep it and the other one doesn't.

"Two days ago, I visited the clinic to see what it was like. I couldn't bring myself to walk through the door. Once I did come inside, I could not believe how many people were here.

"My headache started at two AM. It hurt so badly that I couldn't sleep. I counted the hours until dawn. All I could think about was, 'Get this over!'

"This whole thing is my own fault. If you choose to have sex, getting pregnant is something you have to think about. It wasn't like my boyfriend and I had sex every day, but when we did, we were careful. Well, almost careful, because we did use withdrawal once in a while. For a long time, I couldn't believe this had happened to me. How could I be so dumb? That's why I waited so long."

"Lisa M," Nancy calls. Lisa stands and walks, resolutely, to the bursar, the person in charge of collecting the fees. She hands the teller her mother's credit card to pay for the abortion. The last problem now looms. She doesn't have a letter with her mother's signature giving permission to use the card. The clinic cannot accept the card as payment.

Lisa's head is on fire. What can she do? Neither she nor her boyfriend have any money. She can't put this off any longer. Slowly, Lisa reaches for the telephone, crying. "Hello, Mom . . . ?" She breaks the news, her assumption that her parents would never find out completely destroyed.

When counselors ask if a parent knows whether they are here, many girls insist that their mothers cannot be told. The most often spoken phrases are: "There is no way. . . . She doesn't understand. . . . She will kill me."

Parents who have a bad relationship with their daughters might not understand. The mothers who have a good relationship with their daughters, though, are often perplexed when they learn that their daughters do not feel free to confide in them. The daughters often say that they don't tell their parents because they do not want to disappoint them. Younger teens, the thirteen- and fourteen-year-olds, usually must confide in their families if for no other reason than they do not have anyone else to take care of them. They are children who have little access to information, money, or transportation.

Susan Martinelli, whose duties include the patients with complaints and the tough cases, says she could write a book about some of the people who come to the clinic. "Do you know what many of the girls worry about?" Susan asks rhetorically. "Having their boyfriends wait. They ask, 'How long is it going to be, because my boyfriend is waiting? If he has to be here all day, he'll get mad at me.'

"You're having surgery and he's just sitting up here watching movies," Susan tells them emphatically. "Don't worry about him. Don't let anybody do that to you."

Oftentimes a woman will rely on her partner rather than take her life into her own hands. "'When was my last period?' a patient will ask her boyfriend right in front of me. Wait a minute! It's your period! It's your body. You should know when your last period was."

Mostly, the boys are caring and quiet, but then there are the tough types, the how-long-are-we-going-to-be-here, when-can-she-have-sex-again ones. This makes Susan and her staff really angry.

"Most of the cases are straightforward. But, we've had some strange experiences. On one occasion a detective investigating a credit card theft called the clinic. He had reason to believe that the clinic had some dealings with a fourteen-year-old girl who stole a card from her teacher. Not only did she use it to have an abortion, she bought a great deal of gold jewelry."

Susan told the detective that a few months earlier, a young girl and her friend came to the clinic with an unsigned check. Susan explained that her check was unacceptable. The following week the same girl returned, this time with a credit card. She also had a letter supposedly written by her mother that gave her permission to use the card. "Why does the card have a different last name?" Susan asked the girl.

"My mother is remarried," she was told, which sounded reasonable. Susan felt sorry for her and accepted the credit card. But first, another ID with the patient's name was essential. The teenager produced a school note saying that she was failing chemistry. Susan made a photocopy of the note and attached it to her file.

When the detective came to the clinic with the mother and daughter, he asked for the director. Meanwhile, the girl was disguised: she painted herself with bright blue eye shadow, ruby red lipstick, and she wore a large black hat with a wide, floppy brim.

"Don't I know you?" Randi asked, puzzled, as the incongruous threesome walked by. The girl shook her head, no. Once again, the girl swore to her mother and the detective that she had never been to the clinic. The mother believed her, but Susan knew better because she recognized the girl.

"I've never been here . . . I've never been here. . . ." the girl began to shout. The mother took up for her daughter and began to give Susan a hard time. "How do you know it was my daughter?" she demanded. Susan went to the file and produced the note.

"SHE'S FAILING CHEMISTRY!" her mother screamed.

Susan Martinelli

Susan was a college student in the early seventies when the women's movement was in high gear. In women's studies classes, abortion was a very important issue. At one point Susan took a New Jersey friend to New York for an abortion before it was legal in her home state. "That's where I became certain that the decision about a pregnancy relates to our ultimate right to privacy. And it has to be our decision, ours alone. This, I realized, was *the* women's issue that I could become involved with."

With a degree in social work in hand, her first job was at a family planning clinic. Her second job was a counselor at Metropolitan clinic. When a new clinic was opened, Susan was asked to become its director. Three years later she decided that she could not continue there as director because of the low salary.

"I returned to school for a master's degree in business, and I almost finished it when I said to myself, 'What am I doing? I don't want to do this.' I didn't want to sit behind a desk with a pile of papers and numbers in front of me. I wanted to sit behind a desk with another person in front of me. The work was more important than the salary. I returned to the clinic and I've been here ever since."

Every day Susan is faced with women who are in crisis. Although she empathizes with everyone she counsels, she knows where to draw the line. "I'm not here to solve all their problems. That would be impossible. I'm here to solve this particular problem."

Sometimes, though, a client can get to her, like seventeen-year-old Patricia (name and identity changed). She arrived one morning, all alone. She came by bus. No one, friends or family, knew that she was here. Susan explained that it is the policy of the clinic that a patient is not allowed to have anesthesia, go through a surgical procedure and recovery, unless someone is there to escort them home. Patricia argued that she could handle it, but Susan would not consider it. The clinic policy was clear.

Because Patricia had no choice, she called her sister from Susan's office. "I have something to tell you. I'm in trouble. I'm pregnant." She cried uncontrollably.

Patricia's sister rushed to the clinic. "Please don't tell Mommy and Daddy about this. Please, please, please, they'll kill me. Don't do this to me," Patricia begged.

Susan felt awful. "Sometimes I want to cry with them," she says. "It's hard to be a teenager now, harder than ever."

11

"Do I Have to Tell Them?"

Sarah G, 15 (Name and identity changed)

IT TOOK Sarah twenty weeks before she could admit the unimaginable, "I'm pregnant. There was no way I could tell my parents. Their fifteen-year-old daughter having sex? Impossible." Boyfriend Michael (name and identity changed), who is also fifteen, somehow managed to scrounge up the money needed for a second trimester abortion.

Sarah's curly red hair falls gently over her shoulders. She has creamy skin, and her picture-perfect makeup barely masks puffy green eyes. Behind her is Michael. He is slightly pimpled, skinny, and very tall. His basketball player's long dangling arms protectively encircle her as he kisses the back of her head. Sarah is scarcely aware of him. Discreetly she smiles at Nancy, while Michael does the talking.

Huddled together, under the TV, they fill out her medical chart. Then she goes into the lab for pregnancy and blood tests. After a counseling session, she returns to the waiting room.

Twenty minutes later, when her name is called again, Sarah goes into the examination room, undresses from the waist down, covers herself with a blue cotton gown, and sits on the edge of the examining table. Dr. Poulos, with Nancy acting as his assistant, knocks on the door. Once invited into the room, he introduces himself. "I'm so scared," she blurts out, desperately fighting tears.

He reassures her. "I'm not going to hurt you at all. If anything might hurt, I'll tell you first. Try to relax. I have to see how pregnant you are."

Sarah impulsively grabs at the doctor's hands. Nancy rushes to her side and holds her hand tightly. "Thank you," Sarah stutters, voice cracking. As the doctor examines her, her muscles tense. "I can't believe how frightened I am."

Dr. Poulos asks Sarah a number of questions, including, "How tall are you? Who is here with you? How far away is your home?" And finally, the big question, "Do your parents know about this?"

"Do I have to tell them?" she asks crying.

Dr. Poulos shakes his head, "No," and continues to examine her. He takes an unusually long time to view the fetus. Slowly he moves the eye of the sonogram all around her abdomen to view the fetus and the amniotic sack. The doctor, lost in thought, examines, views the screen, examines, meditates, views the screen, examines. Over and over and over. Nancy has a good idea about why he is taking such a long time. She holds the patient's hand and watches the doctor work. Sarah, who has no idea that Dr. Poulos is giving an unusually long examination, whimpers. Valiantly she tries to relax.

Finally, the doctor says, "You are twenty-one weeks pregnant and we cannot do the procedure here. It's too risky." Nancy reaches for a tissue with her free hand.

The doctor, who has a daughter about Sarah's age, advises his patient that her options are few. It is critical that Sarah understand the ramifications of her indecision. "You don't have any more time left," he says, his manner fatherly. "After twenty-four weeks an abortion can't be performed in this state. You still have the choice to terminate or continue your pregnancy. But, if you choose termination, I'd like to see it done in the hospital. Soon." Sarah is paralyzed.

"Do you have a decent relationship with your parents?" the doctor asks.

"Oh, yes, but I don't want to hurt them."

Nancy steps into the discussion. "Your family will be shocked at first, but, you'll see, they will come through for you."

After some further discussion, Dr. Poulos departs, understanding his patient's need for privacy. She has a great deal to get clear in a short period. "Take as much time as you want to get dressed. Nancy will wait right outside the door in case you need her." He squeezes her shoulder gently.

"Thank you," Sarah says, still sobbing. Nancy tries to reassure her. "If you need me, I'll be right outside."

Nancy's eyes fill with tears as she closes the door behind her. "I don't know why this one has gotten to me so badly. There is something so vulnerable about Sarah that I can't help but respond to her."

The doctor based his decision on a number of factors. One: Sarah's age. Two: Her cervix is very tight because she has not given birth. Three: She is over twenty weeks pregnant. Four: He does not feel comfortable performing this type of abortion, which is riskier, without her parents knowing about it. Dr. Poulos notifies Susan that he cannot perform the procedure. Should Sarah want to go through with the termination, Susan must make arrangements at the hospital immediately.

Once dressed, Sarah is reunited with her boyfriend in Susan's office. Susan describes two procedures available to Sarah. One procedure would be to have a late D & E (Dilation and Evacuation). After twenty-one weeks the laminaria must remain in the patient longer than three hours. A patient has the laminaria inserted, goes home over night, and returns to a clinic the following day to complete the procedure. Metropolitan clinic does not do this type of procedure.

Another procedure is called a saline abortion. In a hospital a patient's abdomen is anesthetized. Then amniotic fluid is extracted by a needle through the belly. This fluid is replaced with a saline solution that will induce labor. The patient actually goes through a labor, including labor pain, and aborts by herself. These are the standard procedures for a twenty-two- to twenty-four-week pregnancy. Labor can last twelve to forty-eight hours. Because of the nature of the termination, and the time it takes, it must be supervised in a hospital.

Armed with this information, the young couple face one another. There are no tears. Sarah is utterly exhausted, totally drained emotionally. Her boyfriend is at a loss. After a few moments he looks at Sarah and says, "I want to tell my parents. I need them."

"Yes," whispers Sarah, "I want my mom."

Dr. Nicholas Poulos

(Everyone refers to the gynecologist, Nicholas Poulos, as "Dr. Poulos," which is a shortened version of his Greek family name, simply because it is too difficult and long to say. I followed suit.)

Nicholas Poulos is handsome, youthful, and dynamic. He believes with a passion in the rights of his patients. "For whatever the reason, or whatever the procedure, the obstetrician–gynecologist must be there for his patient. If I discriminate among those cases I like to treat from those that I do not like to treat, I'm not serving my patient well. I will not treat differently a patient who is planning to have a baby from the one who is planning to have an abortion."

The doctor's official day begins at eight AM when he makes hospital rounds. Immediately afterward he drives down the street to the clinic where he performs pre-abortion examinations and abortions. At four o'clock in the afternoon he begins regular office hours. His working day ends at eight PM, unless he is on call and there is an emergency. The long hours can be tough, but the doctor says that he gets enough satisfaction from his profession that he would not want to change anything.

"All our patients who are more than eleven weeks pregnant are given a sonogram. Sometimes I see pregnancies that are more advanced than the woman has admitted in her medical form. There are various reasons why this happens. One recurrent reason, along with the fear of the expected pain, is that the patient is afraid to admit when she became pregnant. It is not that she lies to me, she lies to herself. She puts her head in the sand, and thinks, 'It's a bad dream that will go away!' It will not!

"There comes a point when the person inescapably realizes that a decision, one way or the other, must be made. New Jersey law provides that a woman can have an abortion until the twenty-fourth week of gestation. At this cutoff point, we're talking about a 500-gram fetus, which is a little over a pound. It is rare that a fetus that small can live outside the womb. If it does live, it won't grow to be whatever you and I know as normal human beings." While the fetus may not be able to survive before the twenty-fourth week, nevertheless, the termination procedure becomes more difficult as time goes by. In the doctor's experience, because young girls often are afraid that an abortion will be painful, they wait. A relatively uncomplicated procedure becomes more complex.

"It is sad when a woman waits so long that she no longer has any choice. Then the decision is made for her by default. I see that again and again."

12

"I Can't Believe This Is Happening to Me"

THIS late morning Dr. Poulos moves briskly between three examination rooms. For patients who are over twenty weeks pregnant, like Sarah, he has a tough decision to make. Should he or should he not perform the procedure?

"Denial often plays a role in a patient's decision. I've heard hundreds of excuses why a patient didn't get her period. 'I broke up with my boyfriend. . . . My uncle died and I thought I was just sad. . . . I've been under a lot of pressure in school.' Meanwhile, the girl is gaining weight, feels nauseous, feels movement, and she has had sex without birth control."

Out of ten teenage patients who Nicholas Poulos examines this Saturday morning, only one patient is in her first trimester. Two patients are far too late to legally have an abortion in New Jersey.

In another examining room, Marybeth (name and identity changed), a seventeen-year-old, is already in place on the examination table. She is sixteen weeks pregnant, early second trimester. As Dr. Poulos inserts a lamineria, he explains everything he will be doing. The verbal preparation decreases his patient's uneasiness and the process is executed without complications. Afterward, Marybeth dresses and returns to her boyfriend, who is in the waiting room.

After two-and-a-half hours, Marybeth's mouth is so dry she can barely speak. Although she has been counseled not to eat, drink, or smoke, Marybeth slips into the women's room to rinse her mouth and swallows a tiny sip of water. That is a big mistake.

To the average person, an operating room has a surreal quality. The four rooms that make up most of the medical floor of the Metropolitan clinic are no exception. The spare, impersonal, narrow hallway connecting the rooms is painted pale green. Gurneys covered in linen and cotton blankets flank each doorway. Nurses efficiently hurry about their duties, which include helping patients in and out of the operating rooms and preparing medical instruments. Everything is sterilized. Each set of instruments is tightly wrapped in green cotton cloth.

Inside each identical room the operating table looks very much like one in a gynecologist's office, except that the stirrups are much higher and the table rotates. In one room a doctor is performing a first trimester abortion, a D & C.

The rate of complications that might occur during an abortion is very low, lower than for operations such as a tonsillectomy, and much lower than for having a baby. Infection is one of the two main complications that can occur during an abortion. Sterile equipment, along with antibiotics, protects the patient from this threat. If there is a problem, for example a high temperature or heavy bleeding, she calls the clinic, where a doctor is on call twenty-four hours a day. The second complication is a perforated uterus. This occurs if an instrument accidentally tears the inner lining of the uterine wall during the procedure. An experienced doctor immediately knows if perforation occurs. This complication is quite uncommon, happening in perhaps one in 3000 abortions. Vital signs are carefully monitored in the operating room. The physician may opt to transfer the patient to the hospital overnight for observation.

Assuming there are no further complications, the uterus heals in a week and the woman returns to the clinic for a two-week postoperative checkup.

Before abortions were legal, some of the illegal abortionists probably sucked out any blood stemming from a perforation and continued with the procedure. A patient could die from internal bleeding.

Marybeth is finally ready to have her procedure. She goes downstairs to the medical floor and knocks on the door. Carla, an operating room (OR) nurse, greets her cordially and escorts her to a curtained-off area in the recovery room. This recovery room consists of a series of beds with curtains around each of them to ensure privacy. As instructed, Marybeth undresses, lays her clothes neatly on the chair beside a bed, and puts on a hospital gown.

"How are you feeling?" Carla asks her patient as she emerges from behind the curtain.

"I'm okay. I felt awful earlier but I took a tiny sip of wa—" She stops short in the middle of her sentence but the nurse picks up fast.

"Water? You drank water?"

"Only a little. . . ."

This was Marybeth's big mistake.

The doctor will not risk aspiration, Carla explains, and the lamineria has already dilated the cervix. Marybeth will have to go through the procedure with a local anesthesia.

The doctor comes into the room, reads Marybeth's medical chart, and assures her that she will be given enough medication to relieve most of the pain.

She looks wretchedly at the doctor and nurse. "I can't believe this is happening to me."

Carla helps Marybeth climb onto the table and then adjusts a green cloth strap to each leg. Very carefully, Carla puts an IV into the vein of her left hand. A tranquilizer drips into the IV. "You're going to feel the effect of this drug in a few seconds. Try to relax."

"How do you feel?" the nurse asks as the anesthetic begins to take effect.

"I'm a little drowsy."

"Are the lights moving up and down?"

Marybeth nods, yes.

The doctor begins by removing the lamineria and inserting a dilator into her vagina. Carla suggests, "Open your eyes and focus out; don't focus in. Talk to me."

"Okay," Marybeth mumbles, her tongue feeling thick.

"You might be experiencing a little pressure," the doctor says. "What I'm doing now is dilating the cervix so that I can get inside to the uterus. You're doing fine."

The doctor continues to use larger and larger dilators. He forewarns Marybeth so that she can get through it more easily. "This is likely to be a little painful. Dilating can cause strong cramps. If you do all right now, you'll be fine. Only a little longer."

The nurse tries to distract Marybeth, asking where she lives and what school she goes to. The mention of school brings out a smile. Periodically, throughout the procedure, the nurse inquires: "How are you doing?"

The doctor is to the point where he uses a curette to scrape the uterus. He attaches a suction tube to remove the tissue. The nurse checks Marybeth's blood pressure as the doctor turns on the machine. After the doctor double-checks the uterus with the curette to be sure that all the tissue is loosened, he turns on the machine once again.

"Are you okay? We're about done," the doctor says.

Marybeth, responding to the drugs in the IV, keeps falling asleep.

"You were very good," the doctor says warmly.

"You were great," the nurse adds.

"Are we finished already?" Marybeth asks, very woozy.

"A little bit of pressure," says the doctor as he carefully removes the instrument. To ward off infection, the doctor swabs the vaginal area with Betadine. Carla casually leans on Marybeth's knee to watch the doctor at work. Human contact feels good.

All of a sudden, Marybeth retches. Carla immediately unties her legs and the doctor holds the pan for her to throw up. "Take a nice, slow, deep breath," the doctor says. "Another deep breath." A large dose of Demerol can make a patient throw up, especially since she hadn't eaten anything.

"Don't hold it in," the nurse adds. Marybeth is through. The nurse checks her blood pressure and pulse rate. The doctor fills out the chart. Carla places a Kotex between Marybeth's legs and wraps soft paper toweling around her bottom. Then she covers Marybeth with the blue cloth gown and gently rubs her shoulders.

The doctor finishes filling out the chart and returns to his patient. "Are you all right?" he asks, kindly. Droopy but smiling faintly, Marybeth indicates yes, thumbs-up.

She wants only to sleep, but Carla gently rouses her. After a few minutes Carla helps her patient off the table and they walk to the recovery room.

Marybeth is led to the curtained sector where she had previously undressed. Her clothing is neatly placed on a chair beside the bed. Before the nurse can say or do anything, she dives into the bed, curls up and goes to sleep. It's over.

Dr. Poulos talks to people like Marybeth every working day. He says, "The message that has to get out is about the importance of birth control. That's the neon light that has to go on for everyone, man and woman." The fact that so many couples refuse to use birth control regularly, thinking pregnancy can't happen to them, is astounding to the professionals who deal with the result of this naive delusion.

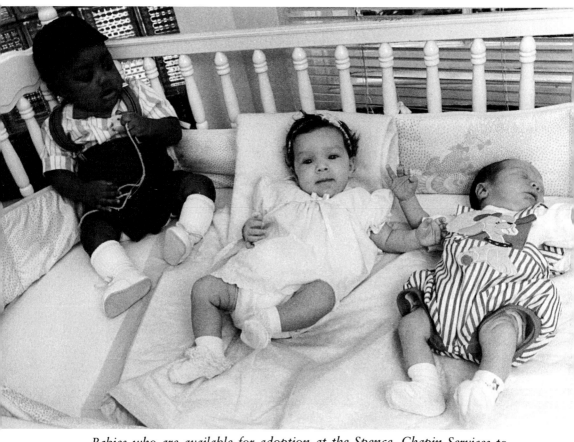

Babies who are available for adoption at the Spence–Chapin Services to Family and Children

13

"I Loved Him Very Much"

AS WILL be seen in this section, in today's society, it is not always acceptable to place your child for adoption. There is generally less stigma from abortion. Choosing the option of having your child adopted is tough. Spence–Chapin, a state-licensed private adoption agency in New York City, is one of many organizations that work with the pregnant woman who is considering this option.

The agency, a nonprofit corporation founded in 1943, is made up of two totally separate departments: the birth parent department and the adoption department.

Alexis (name and identity changed) used the services of the birth parent department.

Alexis, 19

Alexis and Bill (name changed), age 22, dated on and off throughout her high school years. They were known as the "golden couple," admired and envied by their large circle of friends. Last year their relationship became intimate. Though they both knew better, they never used birth control. Like many young women, Alexis simply thought she would never get pregnant.

Toward the end of summer, Bill was preparing to return to his senior year at a college in the Southwest where he is majoring in engineering. He casually asked Alexis when she last had her period. Counting the days backward, they realized that they had sex during the time when she was most likely to become pregnant, two weeks after her menstrual period started. They looked at one another, gulped, and quickly put it out of their minds.

Or did they? Bill went away to college while Alexis, who lived at home, began her sophomore year as a French major at New York University. A few days later Alexis tagged along with a friend who was going to Planned Parenthood to get birth control pills. She decided to take a pregnancy test.

"I will never forget the feeling I had when the nurse walked into the room with the results of my test. When she said that I was pregnant, I almost died. The first thing that flashed through my mind was that there is no way out."

Alexis grew up in a privileged family. Her home is a large, rambling apartment in Manhattan's Upper East Side. Weekends and summers are spent at the family's picturesque cabin in New Hampshire. Alexis is smart, has a model's figure, and is pixie pretty. Here is one girl who seems to have everything. It is quickly apparent that she is down-to-earth and caring. Bill describes her as the kind of person who lights up a room when she enters it.

But that day, the lights dimmed. "I'd always been able to get out of things, but not this time. I knew that this was the beginning of a nightmare."

Telling Bill was so difficult that Alexis decided to break it to him in stages. She called him at school and only admitted that she had gone for the test.

Bill was surprised that she was worried. "Why did you go? Did you miss your period?"

"No, I just wanted to make sure," she lied. "I'll get the results Monday."

Bill knew that pregnancy test results take only a matter of minutes, but he let her lie pass.

Alexis and her best friend went to her cabin in New Hampshire for the weekend in order to decide what course of action to take. "We mostly talked about abortion. My friend reasoned that abortion was my only option. She said, 'You can't have a baby now. You're in college.'

"In our family we often talked in the abstract about the pros and cons of abortion. My mother said that abortion was not something she could ever do, but other women should have the right to make their own decision. I don't know how she would have felt if I did it, though."

Alexis came to the conclusion that abortion was the way to go. "After all, that's what you do when you get pregnant and you don't want the baby. Once it was over, my life would go on and nothing would have changed. If I had the baby, my life would definitely change. All weekend, I thought like this, and just died."

Alexis returned home and finally called Bill with the result of her test. "Well, you're definitely going to get an abortion," he replied. There was nothing more to say about it. Alexis made an appointment with a doctor who was recommended by Planned Parenthood, and Bill wired her the money to pay for it. Everything was in place.

With her friend by her side, Alexis, who is usually very prompt, arrived late for her appointment, too late to have the procedure. Since this doctor only does first trimester abortions on Wednesdays, Alexis had to be rescheduled for the following week.

"At this point I was hysterical. I was so confused about everything. Every single day I talked to Bill on the phone. Every night I cried myself to sleep. I didn't want to have an abortion, but what else could I do? The more I thought about it, the more I became convinced that there were other options. A baby should have both a mother and a father. Even though we were very much in love, Bill was in no rush to get married. So marriage and parenting were out of the question. I was adopted. My birth mother placed me for adoption because she wasn't married. If she had had an abortion, I would not be here. I have a great relationship with my parents. My baby is entitled to have parents who could provide for it the way my parents provided for me. Adoption became a real consideration."

Just before the rescheduled abortion, Alexis called Bill and said, "Forget it. I'm not having an abortion."

"Use the money I sent you and come here. We have to talk," he replied.

Meanwhile, Alexis's family knew nothing about the pregnancy. "They don't believe in premarital sex, so admitting to being sexually active, much less pregnant, was out of the question." She hated lying to them, but this was an emergency. Telling her mother that she was visiting a girlfriend in Boston, she flew to Bill.

"When I told Bill that I would not go through with an abortion, he literally flipped out. He was holding a bottle of soda and he threw it against the wall. He said, 'No, you can't do this! How can you do this to me?' He took my decision as a personal attack. I felt awful. I knew that when I told my parents they were going to flip out, too. Everyone was going to get so angry and it wasn't happening to them, it was happening to me."

After a few hours Bill settled down and became rational. He told Alexis, "You want to have the baby, fine, but you're not keeping it."

"I listened to what Bill had to say. After all, it was his, too, so he had some say in it. But I was the one who had to carry it for nine months."

Even though Bill never agreed with Alexis's decision to go through with the pregnancy, he wanted to be completely involved. He dealt with the practical realities: good prenatal care, no drinking, no smoking, etc.

The following weekend Bill flew home to New York and re-searched everything he could about adoption procedures. He learned about Spence–Chapin.

At Spence–Chapin professional counselors help the birth parents look at their choices and make the best possible decision for them-selves and their baby. They also deal with such issues as medical care, housing, financial aid, and postplacement planning. Through-out her pregnancy, the birth mother is under no commitment to go through with the adoption. Nothing is signed, and no one is pres-sured.

There is no fee paid by the birth mother and she is not paid for surrendering her baby. However, in some cases the agency pays her pregnancy-related expenses. Adoptive parents are charged accord-ing to their ability to pay. Fund-raising events and a substantial endowment by the original founders, Clara Spence and Alice Chapin, help cover the expenses incurred by the agency.

It was Bill, not Alexis, who first called the agency to set up an appointment. A social worker, Susan Lesser, was immediately as-signed to their case. On the phone, Susan asked to speak with Al-exis who happened to be standing right next to Bill, her ear pressed tightly against the receiver. Susan introduced herself and said, "We are here to help you in any way we can to come to a successful resolution of your pregnancy." That simple statement helped Alexis to relax for the first time since she found out that she was pregnant.

Soon thereafter the first meeting with the counselor took place at the agency. Sometimes the meetings take place in the birth mother's home, or wherever else she proposes. The interview, called an in-take, is fact-gathering for all three. Alexis and Bill learned about the agency, including what they could expect if they continued to work with it.

The agency does extensive medical screening, not to screen out a baby, but to be as knowledgeable as possible for the benefit of pro-spective adoptive parents. Oftentimes the agency is unable to obtain information about the birth father either because the birth mother refuses to name him or he refuses to become involved. But in this case biographical information was gathered about both Alexis and Bill.

Susan needed to explore every possible option for them in order to be certain that Alexis was making the best decision for her future and that of the child. She asked the couple lots of questions: "Do you see yourselves as parents? What would it be like to keep this child? Is there a mother or a grandmother who would be willing to take care of this child so that Alexis could finish school? What are your goals and aspirations?"

After the questions, they talked about the present. Prenatal care was carefully described. Doctor's appointments were to be made. Counseling sessions were set up.

Alexis's biggest worry was that people would find out about her pregnancy. She knew that if she continued to live at home, everyone would see what was happening. New Hampshire was out of the question because there would be no one to take care of her and, besides, she knew too many people up there. Susan provided a list of residences where she could live during the remainder of her pregnancy, and Bill offered to visit them with her during Christmas vacation. The agency would pay all the fees for the maternity residence.

Throughout the interview Susan advised Alexis that she was not obligated to the agency in any way. "Abortion is still an option. If you are early on in your pregnancy and have some doubts, we can talk about that. My job is not to talk you into or out of adoption. I'm here to help you in any way I possibly can."

Alexis says that she liked Susan from the first minute she saw her. There was something about her easy-going manner and her quick, friendly smile that helped Alexis to realize that she was in good hands.

By the fifth month the curve of Alexis's belly was quite distended, leaving no doubt that something unexpected was happening to the girl who had everything. Alexis became very, very self-conscious in public. After class one afternoon she took a subway uptown to Bloomingdale's and bought five oversized sweaters in dark colors. "If the *big look* goes out of style, I'm dead," she said to herself.

"Before, my friends and I went to bars or clubs and had a few beers. Now I wasn't drinking anything and my friends found that peculiar. They started asking questions and I stopped looking them straight in the eyes."

Weeks had gone by and Alexis still hadn't told her best friend, who had accompanied Alexis to the doctor's office, what she had decided to do about the pregnancy. The friend kept probing. Eventually, Alexis lied to her by saying that she had an abortion the weekend she visited Bill.

It was amazing that Alexis's parents never suspected a thing about her pregnancy. They never asked a single question. Alexis was convinced that her father would be very disappointed and her mother would go crazy.

Alexis found a million clever ways to keep her parents in the dark. For example, every twenty-eight days she went to the medicine cabinet and threw out a box of unused tampax so that her mother would not suspect that she was no longer getting her period. And she was careful never to be seen getting dressed or wearing anything but "big."

Weeks passed and Susan became concerned over Alexis's failure to tell her parents about the pregnancy. She said, "You're planning to go to a maternity residence. What will you say to your parents? You can't just disappear from the face of the Earth."

"Every time I saw Susan, she asked, 'Have you told them yet? Have you told them?' Bill asked, too. I think eventually I told my parents just to get Bill and Susan off my back. I made sure that I had a plan before I revealed anything. In this way I could tell them that I knew exactly what I was doing and they wouldn't be too freaked out.

"I called my mother into my bedroom and said, 'Mother, remember how you always told me that I should confide in you if I was in trouble and needed help?' My mother had a worried look on her face. 'Well, I'm telling you now that I'm in trouble. I'm pregnant.'

"'What?' she yelled, and literally fell backward onto the bed. It looked as if she had been punched in the stomach.

"Actually she quickly sat up and handled the news a lot better than I thought. She was mostly worried about my getting the proper care and that made me feel loved. And then she wanted to be sure that I understood all my options."

By now abortion was no longer an option because Alexis was in her sixth month. Alexis's mother offered to help her take care of the baby. "I thought about that possibility a lot. Perhaps I could work from nine to five and go to classes at night. But that was ridiculous. When would I see this baby? My mother would be raising him, not me. At times it seemed like nothing could work the way I wanted it to. Telling my mother was such a relief. I had been trying so hard to hide from my parents. It was great not to worry about the kind of clothes I was wearing and stuff like that. I think that they took it so well because I had a plan."

Alexis never talked to her father about her pregnancy. She told her mom to tell him. "My mom said that when she told my dad about what I was going to do, he took it very hard. He said that he would never see his grandchild grow up. It made me feel awful."

Alexis finished the semester and then took the next one off. "My grades were the best grades I ever got. Can you believe that?"

Spence–Chapin invites the birth mother to list, in order of priority, the characteristics she wants her baby's family to have. The majority of the birth mothers request a couple who lives in the suburbs, a nonworking mother, both under forty years old.

The adoption department of the agency chooses one or several families that best meets these requests. "Profiles," consisting of one to two typewritten pages that answer most of the questions about the couple, are given to the birth mother-to-be.

Alexis wanted a couple who had been married for a long time. "I wanted to be sure they had a stable relationship. I'm Catholic so I wanted the baby to go to a Catholic family. I wanted a young couple, but that is hard to find. More couples marry in their late twenties and then they wait to have kids. It was hard to find someone young with all the qualities that I wanted."

Susan gave Alexis profiles of three families. Alexis made copies of them to send to Bill. Independently they agreed on the same couple. "The family that Bill and I chose had already adopted a child through Spence–Chapin. I liked that feature because then my baby wouldn't feel out of place. Besides, I have a little sister who is adopted and I'm really glad about that."

Now that the truth about her pregnancy was out in the open, Alexis could have stayed home for the duration of her pregnancy, but then her friends would have found out about it. "I didn't want that. No one knows except for Bill and my parents." And Bill never told his parents about the pregnancy because Alexis didn't want him to. "I thought that there was no reason for them to know."

Bill flew home on weekends and they visited various maternity residences in the area. At the end of her sixth month, Alexis moved into the residence of her choice. The residence was on a hillside overlooking the Hudson River. "It looked like a castle. There was a pool. I had my own room—a big room, too. We didn't do much at the residence. I was constantly eating. It was the most relaxing place I had ever been to."

Throughout these long, arduous months Alexis had been hiding her pregnancy from friends and family. Now, suddenly, there were people around her who were sympathetic. "The residence was run by nuns, but they didn't act like nuns. I mean, you picture nuns wearing a habit and everything. They wore street clothes and were so caring. They reassured me so many times about what I was doing. They said that I was doing this for the baby's well-being. It was so helpful to talk to them."

At first there were two other young women at the residence, but one had her baby and moved out. Within a month of Alexis's arrival, five girls, ages thirteen to twenty-three, joined her. "I'm still friends with one of the girls. She recently decided to keep her baby. We used to have so much to talk about, because we were in the same boat, but now it's different."

There were diverse reasons why the mothers were placing their babies for adoption. One teenager said, "Just about everyone in my neighborhood has a baby. When I see how they are living I don't want that for myself." Another girl explained, "My parents will be horrified. This is the last thing they will ever want for me." And still another remarked, "My mother will help me, but I don't want to put that burden on her."

There was one girl, a fifteen-year-old, whose parents kept pressuring her to keep the child. That only made her hate the baby. Alexis says that it was really important that this was her own decision. "From day one I loved my baby so much.

"My parents came up to visit me every weekend. They took me out for lunch. More eating! By then I was huge so everyone could see that I was pregnant. That was hard. I look very young and people would stare at my enormous belly. Even though I didn't know anybody in town I was embarrassed. I had aches and pains all the time. The baby became so heavy and it was constantly kicking. Sleeping at night was practically impossible. It kicked me all night. But I didn't blame the baby."

Alexis must have blamed Bill. During nightly phone calls she would complain to him. He'd call and she'd cry. "I thought that he didn't understand how uncomfortable I was. By now I gained so much weight that I looked like a blimp. And I waddled! Me? Waddling?"

When Alexis reached her seventh month one of the Sisters drove Alexis to a nearby town for weekly doctor's appointments. And Susan drove up to the residence for their weekly counseling sessions. Alexis had become quite attached to Susan and looked forward to her visits. "That was the highlight of my week. I could talk to Susan about anything. She always asked me if I was sure about my decision. But she was never judgmental. Susan was a big help."

During the original intake meeting, Alexis had told Susan that she never wanted to meet her baby's adoptive family. When Alexis was about to enter into her eighth month, she changed her mind about meeting the couple. Susan, not at all surprised, informed the adoption department about the change in plans. Once notified, the adopting family said that they would be happy to meet the birth mother.

One month to go! At 3:30 AM, Alexis woke up and felt a sharp contraction. She put on gray sweatpants and a long-sleeved, white T-shirt with wide green and blue stripes. She went to the bathroom and her water broke. "That was a scary feeling. I ran downstairs to the kitchen and told a Sister that my water broke."

The nun started timing Alexis's contractions, which were coming pretty close together. An ambulance was called and soon they were on their way.

"The hospital was ten minutes from the house. As we raced down the road, I said that I had to push.

"The Sister said, 'Don't! Wait till we get there.' The orderly who came with the ambulance checked me and said, 'Oh, my God, the head's coming out! Pull over the ambulance!'

"I gave birth to a boy on the side of the road at 4:30 AM. The cord was wrapped around his head. 'Is he breathing? Is he okay?' I was petrified. Everyone else appeared to be calm considering the situation I was in. And the baby was fine.

"They put him on my chest. He opened his eyes and looked up at me. I will never forget that moment for the rest of my life. He was so cute. I couldn't believe it. It was a miracle."

Once the ambulance arrived at the hospital and mother and child were safely settled in, Alexis called Bill. "Bill, I just had the baby," she whispered.

They talked until a nurse brought the baby into the room for his first feeding. That's when reality set in. "I became such a wreck. I kept sobbing. Susan was on vacation and I wanted to talk to her so badly. I cried about everything but mostly about giving him up. Throughout my pregnancy I knew that I was going to place him for adoption. The parents were picked out and everything. But I thought about changing my mind."

It was painful for Alexis to watch the happy mothers feeding and caressing their babies in the maternity ward. "When I visited the nursery to watch the baby through the window, the new fathers were there, laughing and smiling at their newborns. They'd ask, 'Which one is yours? When is your husband coming?' That was really hard. I wasn't about to go into detail with perfect strangers. Bill flew up to see me. He would not hold the baby because he wanted to keep a distance. He said that he was there strictly for me. I was a little hurt about that. I secretly wanted Bill to say that we should get married and keep him. Susan and I still talk about that. She helped me to understand that you have to have a strong, stable relationship with somebody before you can include a baby. We thought that we had that, but we really didn't. Also, we both wanted to finish school."

Before leaving the hospital Alexis signed a boarding consent form which allowed the agency to place the baby in short-term boarding care for thirty days. The consent form does not give the agency any rights to the baby. The baby lives in the home of one of twenty boarding mothers employed by Spence–Chapin until the surrender papers are signed.

Susan says, "I don't like to rush the surrender. After delivery, the mother's hormones are not normal and she can be depressed. After seeing the baby, the mother could become unsure about her decision. It's not a good idea to do anything too traumatic during that time period. Though some women are ready to sign surrender papers sooner, the thirty days usually gives the mother time to make a considered decision."

During this period the mother can call the agency at any time and say that she has changed her mind. She can also visit the baby at the agency as often as she wants to.

Alexis says that leaving the hospital was the hardest day of her life. Afterward, she worried constantly about the baby's well-being. "I wanted to be sure that he was getting the best care, eating good food, and sleeping in a comfortable bed."

A few days before the surrender Alexis met the adopting parents in a cozy, private room in the agency. "It was hard to meet the people who would be raising my child. When we finally met they were the kindest people. I could feel their warmth. They told me that it was hard for them to meet the mother of the baby and that made me feel better. This turned out to be one of the best things I ever did."

Alexis brought with her a letter that she wrote to the baby. Once she felt that everyone was at ease, she gave the adoptive couple the letter and asked them to give it to him when he was older, if they thought it was appropriate. The adoptive mother told Alexis that she would certainly give the letter to him. And the adoptive father added that they would help the child understand his adoption as he grows up.

"In my letter I wrote that I loved him very much. I explained that I spent a lot of time making this decision, it wasn't a quick decision. I was doing this for him. And I said that I had met his parents and they were great people. I was sure that he would be loved by them. Then I told him that I was adopted and that I loved my parents as real parents. I hoped that he would not forget about me and I gave him a picture of myself. I signed it 'your birth mother.'"

One Month Later

Alexis did not sign the final surrender papers until she was absolutely secure about her decision.

When she signed the surrender papers Alexis had another thirty days to change her mind. "That entire month all I could think about was the baby. Then, when my friend from the residence changed her mind, I considered doing it, too. The month has just passed and it is a relief that I don't have to make another decision. It seemed like a nightmare that went on forever. My life was on hold for nine months. Now I'm working and going back to school. I still worry about the baby but it gets easier every day."

For the next six months Alexis will continue her counseling sessions with Susan. "It is great to have someone to talk to since none of my friends know about the adoption. I can talk to Susan more than I can talk to my mother right now. My parents never saw the baby although they saw pictures of him. These days adoption is kind of a touchy subject in my house. I'm in the process of moving away from Bill. I don't see our relationship going anywhere."

In the future when the child reaches legal age, should Alexis and the young man want to be reunited they must both notify the agency in writing. "At this point I would like to see him again, but I don't know how I will feel twenty years from now when I have my own family. I never tried to find my birth mother. I never even thought about her until this whole thing happened. I'm really happy with my parents and I don't feel the need to search her out.

"This was the hardest thing I ever did, but I know that I made the right decision. I am sure that the baby is going to have a great life, a better one than I could ever give him. Besides, I'm living proof that adoption works."

14

"Being a Single Parent
Is Out of the Question"

Susan Lesser, Social Worker

WHEN Susan Lesser was a teenager she volunteered to work after school at the Hartley Settlement House, a New York City community center. One summer was spent as a counselor at the settlement's camp. She was drawn toward helping other people, especially those less fortunate than herself. Nevertheless, when she went to college she did not major in social services as she had originally anticipated. Instead, she became an English major and minored in psychology.

After graduation she married, moved to Westchester (a suburb north of New York City), and had two children: a son, now eighteen, and a daughter, twenty. Once the children were in school, Susan went to work for the Westchester school district. She became an administrator involved with the selection of candidates for special education, a position that rekindled her urge to help others.

In a few years, Susan joined the Department of Social Services in

Westchester County. Her new job description was right up her alley. She dealt with cocaine-addicted babies, the homeless, foster care, and adoption. While continuing with her work, she returned to school for her MSW (master's in social work). "The job gave me life experience, and the university gave me the tools with which to interpret it."

After Susan's graduation, the family moved to New York City. Armed with her new degree, she applied for a job at Spence–Chapin. Why adoption?

Susan's husband was adopted. "He is one of those individuals who had no interest in searching for his biological family. His family was his family. I was fascinated with that. A few of my cousins were adopted, too, so adoption was never an unknown phenomenon."

At her job interview, Susan asked about opportunities with the adoption department of the agency, but there were no openings. The agency offered her a position counseling birth parents. "This is a tough area to work in, but I wouldn't change it for anything. I learned that I have great empathy for the birth parents and I think that I can be of help. Plus, I like the camaraderie in the department. This is a good match."

Susan works with the birth mother throughout her pregnancy and for six months after the delivery of the baby. Afterward, if she feels that her client needs additional help, she will make referrals. "I'm always available to them, though. If my client still needs me, I won't turn her away. Surrendering a baby is a tremendously difficult decision to make, probably the most profound decision a person will ever make. I feel my client's sense of desperation, misery, and loss. It's a terrible plight to be in. On the other hand, it is also a terrible plight for a single mother to raise a child when she is not yet ready for parenthood. Both she and the child will suffer."

The caseworkers have observed that, more often than not, the birth mother's mother is the most instrumental person in determining what choice will be made. If she tells her daughter to keep the baby, the daughter usually keeps the baby. And conversely, if she says that her daughter should surrender the child, the daughter, who wants her family's acceptance and approval, will usually place the baby for adoption.

Recently, one mother was adamant that her daughter place her baby, and her daughter insisted on keeping it. Susan sensed that the issue was not about the baby, but about power and control. She took the older woman into another room and spoke candidly to her.

"Your daughter might be willing to surrender the baby. But I can tell you right now, if you don't back off, she's going to keep it no matter what you say." Susan's straightforward approach sometimes takes people aback. In this instance the client's mother became calmer, especially after she understood that they did not have to rush into anything.

Although Susan understands and sympathizes with the wishes and feelings of her client's parents, the ultimate decision must come from the birth mother. "She's the one who has to live with the decision for the rest of her life. We want to be sure that *she* is sure that she has explored every avenue before coming to this decision."

Some clients deal with their predicament by detachment. "The clients who continue to deny their pregnancy generally have the more difficult time afterward. We caseworkers do not want a client to wake up when she is thirty-five years old and ask herself, 'Oh, my God, what did I do?'"

During the period when Susan was working with Alexis, she was also seeing another client, Lorna (name and identity changed), seventeen. She was from a very wealthy family from Long Island. During a physical examination before she started college, her family physician diagnosed the pregnancy and called her parents without telling his patient.

Lorna arrived home that evening to find her parents, with stern expressions on their faces, sitting tensely in the living room. They were furious. Even though Lorna had known for some time that she was pregnant, she had put it out of her mind, hoping it would go away. Now, she was shocked into reality as her parents took control of the situation.

The following day, without any further discussion, Lorna's mother took her to see a gynecologist. After a pregnancy test and an internal exam, the doctor confirmed a thirty-two-week pregnancy. It was too late to have an abortion. When Lorna's mother expressed a preference for adoption, the doctor recommended Spence–Chapin.

Judy Greene, the director of the birth mother department, reports that 85 to 90 percent of the birth mothers come to the agency because they are much too late to have an abortion. Many admit that they did not have an abortion because they were afraid that it would be painful. Only a very small percentage of the clients say that they are religiously or morally against abortion. And more often than not, the client will not acknowledge that she is pregnant—even to herself. Judy says, "I have seen clients deny their pregnancy all the way up until the baby is born. It is amazing how many calls we get from hospital social workers after a young woman comes to the emergency room in pain complaining of a kidney infection, an appendicitis, or a strained back. Then she delivers an eight-pound 'appendix.'"

Lorna was a tough case because she was very hard to reach. When she showed no interest in keeping the baby, Susan asked her if she had considered abortion. Lorna explained that she was trying to save money from her allowance to pay for an abortion. By the time she finally saved enough, it was too late. Lorna refused to name or give background information about the birth father.

Susan says, "I explored every possible way to get her to appreciate the significance of what she should be confronting. I couldn't make a dent. Every time I came close to reaching her, something else would drive her further away. The only thing she would admit to was that she wanted her family to love her."

Lorna's parents were the type of people who wanted everything done yesterday. Since they did not want anyone to know about the pregnancy, not even Lorna's sister, they insisted that she move into a residence.

The policy of Spence–Chapin is to encourage their clients to become as involved as possible in the adoption proceedings. Lorna wanted no part of the selection of the adopting parents and certainly did not want to meet them. "I'll leave it entirely up to you to choose," she told Susan.

This was not the first client who did not want to participate in the adoption selection. Susan tried to reason with her. "You may feel that way now, but let's talk about it. Let's examine the possible repercussions."

"There is nothing to talk about," Lorna replied in a bland, monotonous voice.

Susan tried another tactic. "What do you think the child would like to know about you?"

Lorna remained detached. It appeared to be the only way she was able to deal with her situation.

During another session Susan remarked, "I know that you say that you don't care about this baby, the birth father is not around, and this has been a painful time for you. But what happens late at night when you are lying in bed and you feel movement?"

Lorna answered, "I've thought about the prospect of keeping the child, but still, being a single parent is out of the question." At least she was thinking.

Three weeks after Lorna moved to a residence in Pennsylvania, she delivered the baby. While in the hospital she held it briefly, and then never saw it again. Within the month she was off to college. The several calls Susan made to her were never returned. Finally, Susan wrote her that the adopting family had sent a progress letter and photograph of the baby. She asked that Lorna please contact the agency to fetch them. Lorna never responded.

"I think about my own children and see how important the teenage years are. Worrying about a baby is an adult's responsibility, and many adults can't handle it very well either. What does a thirteen, or even an eighteen-year-old, think about throughout a pregnancy? Many can hardly deal with the fact that something is growing inside them, let alone worry about how to take care of it. It's all well and good for us to pontificate about how other people must pattern their lives, but they are the ones who have to live with it."

Take the case of Sheila. . . .

15

"I'm Giving You Up"

Sheila (Name and identity changed), 17

SHEILA says that some of her friends who are teenage mothers are more interested in clubs and parties than in caring for their babies. Frequently they leave their infants with anyone who is willing to take charge. "My friend was working, going out at night, and never had time for the baby. I took care of her son until he was four months old. I got up in the middle of the night, fed him, bathed him, and carried him with me everywhere I went. My mom thought it was not my responsibility. Once I went back to school and there was no one to baby-sit, my friend had to quit her job and stay home. She went on welfare because that was the only way she could support her son."

Though Sheila recognizes that welfare can be a valuable stepping stone for a person who is down-and-out, she's watched friends turn it into a way of life. A life of welfare is not what she wants for herself or her future children.

Therefore, when Sheila became pregnant, she decided to place her baby for adoption. "My friends said that I loved kids too much to go through with it. But I knew it would be best for me and my baby."

Sheila is a vivacious girl who describes herself as one who likes to shout, dance, and have fun. She met her boyfriend, Eddie (name and identity changed), at a dance club. He was ten years older than she, had never been married, but had a four-year-old daughter to support. Eddie was a bit quiet for her. "But he was built really nice. And he was cute."

During her "club period" Sheila went out every night and came home late. Her mother didn't approve of these antics one bit and their close relationship became strained. To ease the tension Sheila moved into her best friend's apartment where the rules were more lax. "I was being wild."

Why Sheila and Eddie did not use birth control when they had sex is the sixty-four-thousand-dollar question. "You won't believe this, but during this time my mother worked for a teen pregnancy organization. I knew all about birth control. I just wouldn't listen to anything she had to say."

After a few months Sheila began to notice that her breasts were growing bigger and she was gaining weight. "I can eat! So I thought it was just one of those things. When I started throwing up every morning, I went to see my doctor." When Sheila's doctor told her of her pregnancy, her first thought was that she was not ready to raise a child. Abortion was out of the question because she was afraid she would feel guilty afterward. "I was much more comfortable with adoption. At least I'd get the chance to know if it was a healthy girl or boy," she reasoned.

With her second thought, Sheila became furious with Eddie. She raced home, grabbed for the phone without taking off her coat, and called him. "I'm pregnant," she screamed.

"What are you going to do?" he asked.

"I don't know."

Eddie never suggested that she have an abortion. In fact, he never suggested anything. When Sheila told him that she was thinking about placing the baby for adoption, he remarked, "Oh, for real? Just do what you have to do."

The lack of concern that Eddie displayed made Sheila rethink their relationship. It wasn't so strong to begin with. "Cute" seemed to be of little importance at a time like this and they broke up soon thereafter.

Sheila did not make the adoption decision blindly. She carefully wrote out lists of reasons why she should keep a baby and why she should not. The "should nots" were longer.

1. I can't provide a good life and a real home for my child.
2. At my age I can't teach strong values and morals.
3. I still have a lot of growing up to do.
4. How can I discipline a child when I still need discipline?
5. If I kept the baby I would be able to get a high school diploma, but who would baby-sit while I went to college? My mother was working. I wouldn't be able to go to school and work.
6. The only way I could care for a baby would be to go on welfare like my friends did. How can I tell my child, "Go to school and make something of yourself," while I sit home, watch the stories on TV, and wait for my welfare check?

Sheila told her mother about the pregnancy. She immediately became caring and sympathetic. Sheila's father was a different story. Afraid that he would be very upset, Sheila begged her mother not to tell him. Since he lives in another city, it wasn't too difficult to keep the secret.

The next step was schooling. How could she continue to get an education while she was pregnant? The answer was a school for pregnant teenagers, similar to the one that Lynne went to on Staten Island. At the first interview with the school's counselor, Sheila announced that she was placing her baby for adoption. The counselor was surprised. All the other girls at the school kept their babies. But she was very friendly and promised to give Sheila extra attention to help her through the pregnancy.

"I knew it was going to be difficult for me to listen to my classmates talk about their dreams and plans for their babies." Rather than live a lie, Sheila decided to be truthful about her choice with her classmates. A speedy emotional reaction ensued: "Oh, my God, how can you give up your baby? . . . You're carrying it for nine months and going through all this trouble just to give it away? . . . You should be put in jail!"

At one point a class discussion centered around Sheila's choice. One girl became so upset that she had to leave the room. "I felt bad about the way the others reacted. I told them that if I was strong enough to listen to their objections and still believe that my decision was the right one, then I knew that I could go through with it."

By now Sheila was five months pregnant. She was showing and was feeling movement all the time. "This is a bad thing for me to say—don't forget I didn't want a baby to begin with—but my pregnancy was a burden. The movement did nothing for me. When I complained, my mom would say that it was a human being. For me, it was just a big burden."

After their first interview, the school's counselor never called Sheila. Two months passed and Sheila's mother called the school to find out why her daughter was not being counseled. Quickly thereafter, Sheila was given an appointment. The counselor was nervous. She asked the right questions to be sure that Sheila made a considered decision, yet she seemed to be prying. That irritated Sheila.

Eventually, the counselor mentioned that Sheila could go on welfare and her mother could help, too.

Sheila exclaimed, "That's not my mother's responsibility. My mom didn't make the baby. Eddie and I made it."

Sheila says that the counselor never asked about how she felt. "All she talked about was what they would do for me if I kept the baby."

Realizing that she could never make this woman understand what she was experiencing, Sheila stopped talking and stared at the ceiling. The counselor did not tune in. "How does the father feel?" she asked. "We can call him. He might want to raise the baby." Sheila did not respond.

Sheila did respond to the counselor's next suggestion because it was really exasperating. "How about sending the baby to your grandmother? She can raise it." Her grandmother raised Sheila so that her mother could get an education. She also raised all of her son's children. This was to be her time to have a life of her own, and for this reason Sheila kept her pregnancy a secret from her grandmother.

"The counselor kept talking and I said nothing. She asked if I had anything else to say. I didn't, so I left. Afterward she never talked to me again. I was glad. When I saw her in the hall, I would avoid her. In her own way she was trying to help, but it just came out all wrong."

Sheila did have some positive support. Her obstetrician arranged for her to speak with the hospital's social worker. The social worker was not at all judgmental and gave her the number of the Spence–Chapin Services. "I was scared to call at first. When I finally made an appointment, my mother went with me for moral support.

"I was impressed the minute we walked into the building. I thought it was going to be one of those dumpy places, but it was very nice, clean, and friendly. I was assigned to a caseworker, Judy. I felt comfortable with her immediately. All three of us went upstairs and talked. We talked about my past and my medical history. I was glad that my mother came along because she was able to answer all the medical questions."

Throughout the pregnancy Sheila went to school, ate junk food, and did nothing else. She quickly gained fifty-seven pounds, which was too much weight for a girl only 5'2". Judy worried that the extra weight and lethargic behavior was the result of depression.

Sheila says, "Judy thought I was depressed, but I was just angry. The control that the baby had over me drove me crazy. I didn't have my body to myself. I had to go to the rest room all the time. Everything revolved around the kid. When I looked in the mirror, I'd think, 'Oh, my God, stretch marks!' Some kids at school actually enjoyed it. They'd say, 'Oh, how cute, I got a new stretch mark over there.' I didn't find that very cute. I hated it. I HATED IT!"

By the time Sheila was approaching her ninth month, she says that she felt like she was a walking invasion. "My body had changed drastically. I had to sleep a certain way because of the baby. The baby could move whenever it wanted to, and I could not. The baby was healthy because of me, and I felt sick because of it. It wasn't fair. I told Judy that I hated having a baby in my stomach. I wanted it out. Like my mother, Judy said that *it* was going to be a human being, but I didn't care. I hated it. She told me that when I saw the baby, I would feel differently. Fat chance!"

During one of Sheila's sessions with Judy, she explained all about the legal documents that needed to be signed after the baby was born in order to place it with the adoptive parents. "Judy read the documents to me first and then let me read them. Then we went through every line together to make sure I understood exactly what I was signing."

The agency will spend time with the birth father if he is willing, but Sheila had not heard from Eddie for months. He never expressed any interest in her pregnancy. With Sheila's permission, Judy called him and asked if he would sign a consent form agreeing to the baby's placement for adoption. Eddie agreed and readily signed.

Judy encouraged Sheila to think about the kind of family she wanted for her baby. During one of her weekly sessions, Judy said, "Write out a 'want list' and include all the characteristics you want the family to have. And list them in order of importance. Then I will try to find the family who is closest to your list."

Sheila thought long and hard about the family she wished for her baby. She wanted a stable, married couple who did not move from city to city like she and her mother had done. "I wanted a family who participated in a religion. It didn't have to be my religion, Catholic. And not one of those weird churches like Satanism. I wanted a family who believed in God."

Sheila preferred a black family to prevent the baby from feeling out of place. Unlike most other teenage birth mothers, Sheila didn't feel the couple's age or professions were major considerations.

After Judy read the "want list," she searched the files and presented a profile of a family who seemed to fit the bill. If Sheila did not respond to this family's portrait, others could be provided. "Luckily, when I read about the family, I loved them. Judy found a couple who had everything I dreamed about and more. I said, 'This is it.' I didn't have to see any more."

On Sheila's due day, just like clockwork, she went into labor. Her mother was with her all the time except when she was talking on the phone with Judy. The social worker does not participate in the delivery. Birth mothers are usually at their most vulnerable during birthing. Often the mother takes one look at the newborn, changes her mind, and decides to keep her baby, which is her right. Because the case worker has spent so much time with her client, her presence at the delivery might exert unintentional pressure on the birth mother to give up her baby. The birth mother must feel no coercion over whether to go through with the adoption.

Unfortunately, as it turned out, Sheila's doctor was not scheduled for delivery room duty the day Sheila was to give birth. The doctor had written out a detailed medical history, including the fact that the baby was going to be placed for adoption.

When the nurse midwife read Sheila's history during labor, she responded emotionally, not professionally. "Oh, how can you do that to your baby? It's your own flesh and blood," she said. "Black babies don't get adopted. The baby will hate you. I'll help you take care of the baby."

In the labor room the nurses talked to one another about Sheila as if she weren't there. "Oh, she's giving up the baby," one whispered loudly to another and they leaned over and stared at her as if she weren't human.

A new shift arrived and the same thing happened. "Think it over. You don't want to give it up. This is your baby," they said.

"I didn't say nothing. I was afraid that they wouldn't help me if I opened my mouth. And, I was in so much pain. I thought, 'Oh, my God, I don't believe they are doing this to me.'"

Labor lasted fifteen hours. "Giving birth hurts too much. When I get married, I want to adopt. I gave birth to a girl. And guess what? I immediately felt differently about her, just like Judy said I would. She wasn't a burden anymore. She was beautiful."

Sheila was wheeled into a large cheery room with five other new mothers. At feeding time, the others were given their babies, but not Sheila. "How come you didn't bring my baby?" she asked the nurse.

"We thought that since you are giving her away for adoption, you wouldn't want to see her." This nurse reminded Sheila of Nurse Ratchet from the movie *One Flew Over the Cuckoo's Nest.* "With all the great nurses around, it was just my luck to get a Nurse Ratchet."

Finally, the nurse brought the baby in and Sheila fed her. Then, when Sheila's mother wanted to see her granddaughter, for some unexplained reason, the nurse would not let her. Sheila and her mother did not know how to deal with such mean-spirited treatment.

The following day Judy visited her client in the hospital. She drew the hospital curtain around the bed to give them privacy as they spoke. Sheila told her how the nurses were treating her. Judy was not surprised by the nurses' behavior. She had witnessed it all too often. Many people, even with professional training, have a difficult time dealing with a mother giving up her baby, despite the fact that it is beneficial for the child.

Before leaving, Judy called the hospital's social worker to come down and make sure everything was okay. The "non-judgmental" social worker was on vacation. Sheila says, "I thought the new one was going to be professional like Judy and the previous one."

When the social worker arrived, she did not shut the curtain. She talked so loud that the women in the other beds did not have to crane their necks far in order to hear the conversation. Sheila was asked if she was comfortable about placing the baby. After Sheila's affirmative reply the hospital's social worker said, "Then there is no need to have a name for her," and she walked out.

The other mothers in the room looked at Sheila as if she had three heads. "I felt so bad that I shut the curtain to be alone."

By the third day Sheila was about to be discharged. The nurses finally allowed Sheila's mother to see her granddaughter. She held and fed her, and told Sheila she looked just like her when she was a baby. "Judy told me that my mother was taking it harder than I was. This was her first grandchild."

The plan called for Sheila to be discharged first and then Judy would come and take the baby to boarding care. Before she was discharged, Sheila fed the baby for the last time. "I was feeling so bad that day. I thought, 'Oh, my God, it's going to be final.' When the nurse brought in the baby, Sheila was not allowed to close the curtain. She bent down to whisper to her daughter. "I love you. You probably won't remember this day, but somehow you will always have it in your head. When you get older you might not understand why I did what I did. We will always be together in some way." Sheila was explaining her reasons for placing her when the nurse marched in.

"It's time for the baby to go," she said. Sheila looked up at her curiously. The other mothers were still playing with their babies. When the baby was taken away, Sheila says that she must have gone into shock. She got out of bed, went into the bathroom, washed, dressed, and walked out. Sheila's mother found her walking toward the front door and asked where she was going.

"I don't know. I just feel so bad." Her mother hugged her and promised that everything was going to be okay. "I didn't want to go back in that room and see all the babies, so my mother arranged for my discharge while I waited in the lobby."

After giving birth, students do not return to school for ten days. Sheila sat around the house, studied a little, and watched television. "Everything on TV was about adoption or teenage pregnancy. It was very weird. I didn't want to go back to my school because I knew that the other kids would ask me all kinds of questions. But I had finals to take and I was determined to finish the year with a good grade average. I asked Judy to call the teachers and tell them not to pressure me when I came back."

Everyone was tense on Sheila's first day back at the school. The teachers tried hard to make her feel welcome, but their greetings seemed forced and contrived. Such remarks as, "Oh, you look nice" and "Are you going to be in our talent show?" sounded fake. So long as they didn't ask questions about the adoption, she was able to handle the tension.

"I guess the school's counselor was feeling a little bad, too, because she called me into her office. First, she said, 'You look nice.' Then she asked me how I was dealing with the adoption. The question didn't bother me too much because it was her job to ask me that.

"Our talk was going along fine until she said, 'You know that every time her birthday comes along you're going to feel bad.' I told her that I knew that I probably will feel bad, but I have things to do with my life. Then I told her all about my plans to go into the military, but I don't think she was listening.

"The counselor interrupted me, 'Still, every time her birthday comes you might get that feeling.' I rolled my eyes and looked at my watch." The counselor smiled sweetly and suggested that if Sheila ever needed someone to talk to she could always come to her.

"Why would I want to talk to her? Besides, I have Judy. I would trust my life to Judy."

This was the last conversation the school's counselor ever had with Sheila. From then on it was simply "hi-bye."

In spite of the pregnancy and the tension, Sheila passed all her courses with As and Bs. She was happy that everything was over and she would no longer have to go to a school with pregnant teenagers. There was one more affair that had to be finalized: signing the surrender papers for the baby.

Sheila visited her daughter at the agency two times. "I only saw her twice because I didn't want to make a relationship that wasn't going to continue. During our first visit I told her again everything I had already said in the hospital, only this time I felt more comfortable about it. I took pictures of her. Judy took some pictures of us together. I wasn't crying this time, because I knew that she was being well taken care of."

Sheila's mother came along for their second visit. The grandmother was amazed at how big the baby had grown. Judy stayed with them for a short while and then left them alone with the baby. Sheila's parting words to her daughter were about her hopes and dreams for a happy future. She said, "I'm giving you up so that we can both have a better life. If I sit around and do nothing worthwhile, you'd probably think that I might as well have kept you. But I'm doing this so that we both have a chance to improve ourselves. I want you to be proud about this decision and say, 'Hey, it was for a good cause.'"

Sheila does not want to intrude in her baby's life. She understands that the adopting mother is now the baby's mother. "I'm her mother by birth, but she's the one who will take care of her. If my daughter does find out about me, I want her to know that I was able to achieve something. I hope she does, too."

Four Months Later

Once the papers were signed and everything was final, Sheila told her grandmother, who lives in Trinidad, about her pregnancy and the adoption. "My grandmother took it hard. She said that she would have taken the baby. I did not want to do that to her."

Sheila and her mother are closer than ever. "We worked out all our problems. Besides, the only people we have is each other. It took a pregnancy to make me realize that. I know that this decision was the right one for me. Having a baby is too much responsibility. Some of the kids at my school were on their second or third child. Adoption was never talked about at the school. Neither was abortion. The teachers did talk about contraceptives, but no one paid any attention.

"The girls who had had their babies when I had mine are already out partying. How about the baby? I think it's a big mistake for parents to take care of their children's babies. They baby-sit, spoil it, and the teenager never learns to be a responsible parent. They go back and have another one because they didn't have to do nothing for the first one. It's a never-ending cycle."

16

"I Wanted the Best for You"

JUDY GREENE says, "So many people see adoption as selfishness on the part of the birth mother. One of the things we try very hard to get across to our birth mothers is that adoption is a caring act, not a selfish one. They are providing for their child, which is exactly what a good parent does. Sometimes the birth mother feels that she is abandoning her baby. We don't see it that way. Most of the time these women are loving, tender, pained people who are doing the best for their babies. It is nothing to be ashamed of. It is important to help the birth mother feel good about what she is doing.

"I will ask, 'What does a good parent do?'

"A good parent sacrifices for their child, provides for him, gives him love, stability, stimulation, and material things. Adoption can provide that."

Because this is an important decision, the agency wants the birth mothers to feel secure. Judy says, "This choice will affect them for the rest of their lives and we want them to be as prepared as they possibly can be. We try to answer all their questions. Sometimes we arrange for them to speak with other young women who have placed their babies.

"Most birth mothers write letters to the baby. Generally the theme is the same: 'I love you, don't hate me, I wanted the best for you.' The letters are very moving."

Once the birth mother has been counseled and has worked out the issues, chosen a couple from the profiles, and perhaps met the couple, she is usually ready to make a considered decision. If that decision is still adoption, the process of surrendering the baby begins to fall into place.

Susan Lesser advises every client not to sign the surrender papers unless she is absolutely certain that she wants her baby to be adopted. This sometimes takes several weeks before she makes the decision either to sign the papers or take her baby home.

Adoption rules vary substantially from one state to the next. In New York State, the birth mother has a short grace period to change her mind. However, the right to reclaim the baby is uncertain. The birth mother's lawyer and the adopting couple's lawyer must go to court, along with their clients, and argue for the custody of the child. The agency is no longer involved in this kind of proceeding. A judge then determines who will be the most appropriate parent, that is, what is in the best interests of the child. That's risky business for the birth mother.

Spence–Chapin does not recommend that the birth mother see the baby and sign the surrender papers on the same day. Both experiences can be very emotional. On the other hand, the birth mother may need that last moment with her baby. It can be reassuring for her to be able to say to herself, "I saw the baby at the last possible moment and he or she was okay." After counseling, the agency goes along with the wishes of their client about how to say good-bye to the child.

The transfer of the baby to the adopting parents occurs at the agency. A caseworker from the adoption department of the agency delivers the baby to the family. The birth parent caseworker is rarely invited to the transfer. Susan says that the transfer is usually a very emotional time. She only attends it if the birth mother so requests and if the adoption caseworker invites her.

In an unusual occurrence, Angelica (name and identity changed) was present when her baby was transferred to the adopting family. What made this adoption proceeding even more unusual was that Angelica insisted upon handing the baby over to the adopting parents herself. One can imagine how very painful this usually is for a birth mother.

Angelica, 17

Angelica was from an upper-middle-class family in Connecticut. The birth father, Lenny (name and identity changed), age nineteen, was from Pennsylvania. It was Lenny who contacted the agency when Angelica refused to have an abortion. Susan says, "Angelica's case was similar to Alexis's in that she would have married Lenny if she had the opportunity. Although they were a wonderful, loving couple, Lenny insisted from day one that he was not getting married."

Unlike most clients, Angelica didn't keep the adoption a big secret. Her college friends knew about it and they were very supportive. Both Lenny's and Angelica's families knew about the pregnancy. Angelica's parents felt that a baby would ruin her life. Though they like Lenny very much, marriage never entered into their discussion with their daughter. When the couple first looked at their options, Lenny's mother offered to raise the baby. Neither of them wanted that. When Angelica's grandmother offered, they said "no." Adoption seemed to be the way to go.

Angelica's mother accompanied her daughter to the intake meeting. During the meeting, the mother asked Susan if her daughter would ever get over what she was about to do. Susan wanted to be as honest as possible. She said, "No one can answer that question. I think she'll resolve it, but it isn't going to be easy. There will always be some loss."

Seven months after her first intake meeting, Angelica delivered a beautiful baby girl.

On the day of the surrender, Angelica arrived at Spence–Chapin with her parents and Lenny's. The parents came along to support their children. They did not want to meet the adopting couple, however, and sat downstairs in the lobby's waiting room.

Angelica and Lenny walked into the room to meet with the adopting couple seated in the center of a black leather couch. The couple immediately jumped up to greet them. Everyone, including Susan, was very nervous. Angelica's lip quivered as they all fumbled to shake hands. At first there was anxious giggling on all sides. In a short while everyone settled down and started talking.

The meeting lasted about an hour. Lenny let Angelica do most of the talking. Even though the atmosphere was somewhat strained, everyone tried to be as open and honest as possible. Angelica told the couple that she had been on an emotional roller coaster all year. She mentioned that some people's insensitive remarks about her decision made her question the wisdom of it all. The couple later said that they were very moved by Angelica. They admired her courage and understood what a difficult decision it was.

Adopting parents and birth parents can arrange to share letters and pictures. Mailings are carried out via the agency to ensure confidentiality and anonymity. Usually the letters continue until the time of the adoption finalization, from six to eighteen months. After that, most of the families are not comfortable with more contact. Angelica and the adopting couple agreed to share letters and photographs up until the finalization of the adoption.

When the time came to transfer the baby, the adoption caseworker brought the baby into the room. She gently handed the tiny infant to Angelica. With tremendous resolve Angelica handed her daughter to the couple. Everyone, except Angelica and her cooing baby, was crying.

Angelica turned, put her arms around Lenny, and walked out. Once outside, she broke down and cried. Susan, who had been crying, too, hugged her clients tightly. The threesome returned, arm in arm, to the lobby where their parents were waiting.

Angelica threw her arms around her mother and father and said, "I'm so sorry for all the pain I've given you."

Susan says, "That broke me up. It was remarkable that a girl so young could think of another person's pain at such a moment."

The staff of the Adolescent Pregnancy Program, North Central Bronx Hospital

17

"I Love Pregnancy"

LIKE the waiting room at the Metropolitan clinic in New Jersey, the Adolescent Pregnancy Program at North Central Bronx Hospital in New York is packed with people. The hospital services a broad ethnic community, predominately Hispanic, who are struggling to realize the American dream. Pregnant teenagers, usually accompanied by their boyfriends and often toting another baby, wait, knit, chat, or sit quietly with blank expressions on their faces.

This program includes a multidisciplinary team of professionals who care for the physical, mental, and psychosocial needs of their patients. Because the mothers are themselves in a pediatric age group, a pediatrician tends to their health and the health of their babies. A midwife is in charge of the prenatal care and delivery. Social workers, health care workers, psychologists, and nurses round out the group.

When teenagers first come to the clinic, they are often ambivalent about what to do about their pregnancy. There are some who are obliged to carry their pregnancy to term and others who feel that they have to have an abortion. An important part of this program is that the staff is very supportive of the teenagers' decisions.

Maude Joseph walks briskly down the hall, warmly greeting every teenager by first name, cuddling the newborns, and softly imparting practical information whenever she gets a chance. "There is so much these children need to know, and so little time to teach it to them," she says, snuggling Melissa Figueroa's six-month-old baby boy, Chaz Michael.

Mrs. Joseph, as everyone calls her, is the program's administrative coordinator. She brings to her job a varied background as a registered nurse and a midwife. Before coming to this hospital she worked with pregnant teenagers for ten years. Mrs. Joseph is the hub of the clinic. The various spokes of the program pass through her first. Calm and always smiling, she seems to know everything that's happening. Mrs. Joseph appears to be in five places at once.

In a large office that doubles for an examining room, Dr. Emelyn Quijano, a pediatrician who is the medical director of the program, is examining baby Erica, the daughter of thirteen-year-old Nancy Vargas. Because Nancy had been feeding her baby spicy Spanish food, Erica was having intestinal problems. The doctor explains that she is too young to eat adult food. Nancy offers an explanation. "I don't like it when Erica looks at me when I'm eating. I have to give her some food," she groans while her boyfriend, Hector, kisses their daughter.

Next door in a smaller office that also acts as an examining room, Sylvia Blaustein (affectionately called Sylvie) is the only midwife assigned to the teen clinic. Sylvie will be the teen's midwife throughout prenatal care, up until the delivery. Then, if she is on duty when the baby comes, she will do the delivery as well. Usually, though, a baby waiting to be born does not take into account Sylvie's delivery schedule, and one of the other twenty midwives at the hospital does the delivery.

"Jackie?" Sylvie calls out for her next patient.

Jackie, sixteen, gets up and follows her into the examination room leaving her boyfriend, George, seated in the waiting room.

"What's that scratch on your face?" Sylvie asks, scrutinizing her patient. Jackie explains that a friend scratched her in the face and stomach. "She's a friend?" Sylvie questions, incredulously.

"Not anymore," says Jackie.

Seated at her desk Sylvie reviews Jackie's medical chart. Jackie, meanwhile, is fascinated with the sonogram pictures of her uterus, which show the growing fetus. "This is the opening of your womb," Sylvie explains, "and that's the cervix. Your cervix is what's going to open up for you to have your baby. Your baby is fed through the placenta via the umbilical cord. Your placenta is in the back part of your uterus.

"The technicians doing the sonogram saw the baby's heart beating. There is a normal amount of fluid, that's the amniotic fluid surrounding the baby in the womb where it swims around. Everything is perfectly normal. Your baby is about sixteen weeks."

Sylvie adjusts her birth calculator, a plastic wheel with numbers around it that figures due dates. "Your baby is due September fourteenth but hardly anybody delivers right on their due day. It will be a week earlier or a week later."

"That means the baby will be a Virgo, right?" Jackie inquires.

Sylvie smiles. "I don't know, my wheel doesn't tell me that."

"Yep, he'll just make it. A Virgo, like his father."

It is important for a pregnant woman to gain weight by eating the proper foods. That's hard for most teenagers. Sylvie teaches the mothers-to-be which foods give the right nutrients and which do not. Soda and junk food are wrong. Milk products and green and yellow vegetables are right. A proper diet is one of Sylvie's major battles because most teenagers eat mainly junk food.

"Now, I'm a little bit worried about your weight. What do you eat in a day, Jackie?"

"All kinds of things," she replies, a little hesitantly.

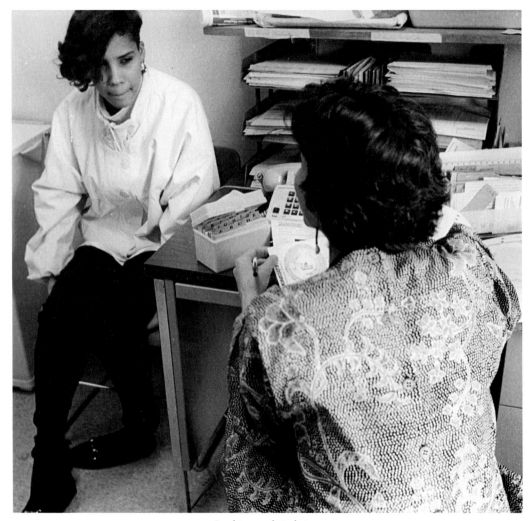

Jackie and Sylvie

"What did you have for breakfast today?"

"Spanish food."

"That's great. Spanish food is great," Sylvie's enthusiasm erases Jackie's misgivings. Her defenses drop.

"Yes. I ate one bowl of rice and nothing since."

Sylvie's shoulders droop. Jackie needs to eat much more frequently. "I want you to pick three days to write down every single thing you eat and we'll go over it together."

When Jackie reports that she can't swallow her vitamin pills, even the very important iron pills, Sylvie checks the chart to see if the lab results show enough red blood cells. The count is much too low. "You need to take the iron pill three times a day. And you need to take them with juice, don't take them with milk."

"That's what I take them with, milk," Jackie wails.

"You're not taking them right!" Sylvie hollers and she squeezes Jackie's cheeks. "The iron doesn't get absorbed into your system when you take them with milk. We're striking out with the vitamins," she sighs. "It sounds like you're eating good food, but not quite enough of it. Be real honest and write down every single thing you eat. And how much. Don't just write down rice and beans, tell me a cup or two cups." They laugh together. Sylvie doesn't push too hard in order to get her point across. She believes that her patient wants to do what's best for her baby.

Jackie tries to make up for her low marks on vitamins. "I drink a lot," she says proudly.

Sylvie perks up. "What are you drinking?"

"Soda."

Sylvie throws up her hands. "Don't drink soda. It isn't good because it has too much sugar. Drink juices, milk, even water."

"I drink all kinds of things."

"Are you drinking milk?"

"No, not much, just with the pills."

Jackie is determined to prove that she is taking care of her baby. "I eat oranges, apples."

Sylvie smiles. "And do you have yellow vegetables?"

"I eat vegetables. And I eat potatoes."

Sylvie moves on. "It's better to eat a lot of small meals rather than one large one. Eat your three meals and have a snack in the middle of the day and again before you go to bed." Foodstuffs affect the development of the baby. The proper growth of the baby's bones, teeth, tissue, and brain is dependent upon the foods that the mother eats.

During the physical exam, Sylvie invites Jackie to listen to the baby's heart beat. She directs her stethoscope below the belly button and tries to find the place where the heartbeat is heard the loudest. After Jackie listens, Sylvie says, "Your belly is growing nicely. The only thing I'm worried about is the weight gain."

"I don't want to gain weight," Jackie moans.

"Yes, you do want to gain weight." Sylvie smiles at this remark, one that she has heard many times before from her teenage patients.

"When I'm with George, I make my stomach look bigger." And Jackie shows how she can protrude her belly. "He likes looking at it. He says, 'Look how big it is,' and I say, 'I know, and it's gonna get bigger.'"

"It's going to get much bigger," Sylvie agrees.

"Oh, no," Jackie does an about-face. "I don't want to look funny." Sylvie cracks up, and so does Jackie.

Sylvie: Nurse Midwife

"I love life! I love pregnancy! That's why I'm a midwife." Sylvie is the daughter of holocaust survivors. Her parents were not actually in the death camps—they met in a refugee camp—but the rest of her family were killed. "Children of survivors get all kinds of conflicting messages," she says. "We're supposed to make up for the losses in our parents' lives. A very intense relationship unfolds between holocaust survivor parents and their kids. The loss of our extended family dominated my childhood. Perhaps that is why I've always been attracted to joyous experiences." For Sylvie, birth is the most miraculous event in the whole world. "When I feel a baby in a woman's belly and tell her that her baby is growing beautifully, I get excited. When she hears me, she gets excited, too."

Sylvie's parents are supportive of her chosen profession, even though they had different ideas about her future. Her father wanted her to enter the academic world. A professor at Columbia was his dream for his daughter. Her mother would have preferred a career in the performing arts. As a child, Sylvie's "joyous experiences" revolved around the magic of dance. She attended ballet school and was chosen to play Clara, the lead in George Balanchine's *The Nutcracker,* at the New York City Ballet.

After college Sylvie taught dance, both modern and ballet, in Upstate New York. She is married to a social worker/therapist and has two daughters.

Sylvie's first child was delivered by a midwife, She became enthralled with the process. After her second daughter was also delivered by a midwife, Sylvie revised her goals. She replaced her toe shoes and leotard with a stethoscope and white hospital jacket.

A year and a half in a master's degree program in nursing came first and then a year as a delivery nurse at Jacoby Hospital before she became eligible for midwifery school. She attended Columbia University for still another year and a half and got a master's degree in midwifery. During that period her children attended the Purple Circle Day Care Center during the day and her family helped take care of the kids while she studied at night.

To date, Sylvie has delivered two hundred sixty babies. "I've enjoyed every single one of them. When you see a birth you won't believe it. It's so incredible. People ask if it ever gets routine. Not for me. There are births that are more pleasant than others and there are births that are more routine than others. I might get along better with one mother than with another. There are all kinds of variables; for example, medical complications make me nervous. But every single time I see that baby's head, I get goose bumps.

"That's not to say that I don't worry. I see my girls throughout their pregnancy, and if I'm lucky, I'm there for their delivery. But I worry about what's going to happen to them later. Into what kind of environment will they be bringing their babies? Some of the girls do beautifully. Some are determined to do better for their babies than their own experience. But these mothers are children themselves, and they have not yet gotten what they need."

During the initial prenatal visit, Sylvie makes it crystal clear how often a future mother must have a checkup. She explains what foods should be eaten, what to expect physically and emotionally before, during, and after the birth.

Sylvie asks her patients if this was a planned pregnancy, and the embarrassed response usually is that it was not. When a young girl tells Sylvie that the baby was planned, she wants to know why. Sylvie says, "I worry about the ones who have planned it. Why would a fifteen-year-old want to have a baby? Usually those are the girls who are very, very lonely, and have an image of someone who is going to love them and who they will love. It isn't as easy as that."

Sylvie's patients are only those teenagers who have decided to continue their pregnancy. She doesn't deal with abortions at all. There are times, though, when an ambivalent patient, who is early on in her pregnancy, will raise the possibility of an abortion with her. Those patients are given counseling by Sylvie and a social worker and, if they choose termination, the proper referrals.

According to Sylvie, many of her patients are those who are the most depleted by life. She can't make up for the losses in their lives, but she can make them feel better about taking care of themselves. Although she doesn't consider herself a replacement parent, she supplies her patients with the nurturing and the respect that they might never have had. Often that extra personal attention will produce a more responsible mother and a healthier baby.

"For the most part, the girls attending this clinic didn't take responsibility for their sexual activity, but they take care of those babies inside of them. Afterward, they learn how to look after the baby. The boys don't.

"I must admit I have a hard time with the boys, not the girls. Even though I know that it is wrong to think this way, I blame the boys a lot more than the girls, because I know that they are not going to be raising those babies. The reality is that they are not.

"As time goes by, the girls have a pregnancy to deal with. They entertain dreams about getting married and having a beautiful house of their own. That's not going to happen. There is a big difference between supporting the girl through the actual birth and taking care of a baby afterward. These are not boys who are going to do that for them. I know that some of the partners are wonderful, right there breathing with them, feeling for them when they are in pain. But others are very detached. They simply drift off and a wall closes. I'm going to try to become a little more tolerant of the boys."

George and Jackie

18

Jackie and George

JACKIE and George are neighbors in the Bronx. Three years ago, when she was thirteen and he fifteen, Jackie would watch George fooling around with his friends on the corner. She liked what she saw, and, when she asked questions about him, she liked what she heard, too. She says, "I liked everything about him and so we started going together. But I wouldn't sleep with him." One day, Jackie says, "We started messing . . . and . . . it got serious. After that one time I never saw his face again."

For months Jackie sat by her window, hoping to see George walk by, and when he did, she ducked. She certainly didn't want him to see how much she cared.

A couple of years passed. Jackie dated a few other guys but she was not serious with any of them. One afternoon George's younger brother knocked on her door. George wanted to speak to her. Jackie went to his apartment and everything started all over again.

"Three years ago I really cared about him, but I started to forget him. And now I like him even more."

One day, after George returned home from his after-school job delivering groceries, Jackie marched into his apartment. "I think I'm pregnant," she announced.

"At first I didn't believe her," George says. "You know, everybody says that, that they *think* they're pregnant." He told her to check it out before they got all upset. Jackie informed George that if in fact she was pregnant, she would get an abortion. He was relieved.

When Jackie's pregnancy test came back positive, she changed her mind. Jackie says that when she was told that an IV would be inserted in her vein, as part of the procedure, she was afraid that the needle would hurt. Besides, she liked the idea of carrying George's child. George looked at her, baffled. "What happened to the abortion?" That response did not sit well with Jackie. She became indignant. "If you don't want to be with me, fine, leave."

George started sweating. He says, "When I heard the news, my jaw went to the floor. All kinds of things rushed into my head: money, Pampers, future, house. I thought, wow, I'm not making enough to support myself. I haven't graduated high school. I'm going to take my college entrance test next week. How can this be happening to me?"

Infuriated, he called her dumb and stupid. "I laid it all on her. But I have to take some responsibility," he now admits.

How it happened was very simple. Jackie refused to go on the pill and George ran out of condoms. "With my bad luck, I ran out at the wrong time."

George says he's still too young to be a father. There are so many things he wants to do, including getting a high school diploma and pursuing a music career. "The news that I'm having a kid is shocking," he says.

Soon George and Jackie found that they were constantly arguing over the dumbest things. George said that Jackie had to have everything her own way. When he tried to give his point of view about anything, she jumped on him, saying, "No, no, that's not right." She became irritated over every little thing. And to top it off, she became extremely jealous. Jackie, on the other hand, felt that she could not count on George to be there when she needed him. He was always somewhere else. And she was convinced that George was going to cheat on her.

The only thing the couple did agree on is that they wanted a boy. George has dreams of the good life for his son. "I want my son to hang out with a positive crowd, not a bunch of down-and-outs who cut school and do drugs. They are the ones who always criticize life. Go with the positive people who talk about a better life, helping others, making money."

While George was growing up, his father wasn't around much. He swore that his child would never be fatherless. Even if his relationship with Jackie doesn't work out, George reasons, he will take care of the child. "I figured one way or another I'd better stick around. My father was never open with me. Every week he'd visit me. I couldn't wait to see him because I had so many things I wanted to ask him. But when he came, it was hard for me to talk to him. I'd like my child to be able to talk to me about anything."

Curiously, Jackie's number-one complaint about George is that he is not open with her. "He doesn't tell me how he feels about the baby, about me having the baby. He doesn't talk to me, really talk."

George says, "I like to be alone. She's pregnant and I don't want to hurt her, but she's taking control of my life. I feel like I'm in prison."

George talked to his mother about his predicament. She tried to help him understand that girls often become very emotional when they are pregnant. "But Mom," he complained, "I feel like she has handcuffs on my arms."

"She does," his mother said.

George's Side

"Boy! Am I in a trap. I'll just have to take it one day at a time until the baby's born. I swear that I will be there for the baby, my son.

George

But Jackie is another story. I'm trying my best, but I'm not going to push a bad thing.

"Jackie dropped out of school and is looking for a job. I worry about her education. In case we don't work out, and right now I see that we won't, Jackie is going to need a good education to get a decent job. She can't be dependent on Mom and Pop forever. With no education, she will be stuck. I try to talk to her about it, but she won't listen to reason."

Back home, George's mother tried, for the zillionth time, to explain that a pregnant woman needs understanding and support. "I try to be understanding and do things her way, even when I disagree with her. I only hang out with one friend," he pleaded, "and still Jackie gets mad. She's always here. Every day she's with me. It's boring. What does she want? Total control? Have I no say about my life?"

Jackie's Side

"This is what I think: He doesn't like being seen with me. The only thing we do together is watch movies at his house. He won't go out. He won't go dancing. If he don't have money, that's okay, I can always get some. When I offer, he won't take money from me. He says it's not right. If one of his friends invites him to go dancing, he goes right away. When I ask him, 'No!' I see him here in the hospital, and that's it.

"Last week, he invited me to the movies. We set a date for Thursday night. I was so happy, I counted the hours. Thursday came and I waited, but George never showed up.

"I can't stand being treated like this. I love him. I love everything about him, except of course, the way he treats me."

Jackie's behavior upset her dad. He told her, "Let him come after you, don't go after him. Every time you fight, you go to his house, he never comes to our house."

Jackie whined, "I just want him to pay a little bit of attention to me. He never talks about the baby. Never!"

Jackie was three weeks late for her monthly clinic appointment and Sylvie called to find out why. Jackie explained that she had had another fight with George. She thought that George was paying too much attention to his sister. After sharp words between them, she stomped out of his apartment, totally frustrated. Before leaving, she smashed his telephone.

On happier occasions, for example, Valentine's Day, George had given Jackie a large heart filled with chocolates and a smaller one with "I love you" written on the box. For her birthday he bought her a beautiful new suit. But these times seemed forever ago. After this latest fight Jackie ran into her bedroom, slamming the door behind her. She tore apart the hearts and threw the chocolates into the garbage. Then she went after the suit, ripping it to shreds and pouring red nail polish all over it. "When I'm upset I do crazy things. I took the empty heart boxes and the suit to his house and left it on the doorstep."

Late that night when George returned from work, Jackie telephoned and demanded to speak with him.

He grabbed the telephone from his mother. "I don't want to speak with you. I don't want to see you. You crazy." And he hung up.

George's family always leave the front door unlocked so that his younger brother and sister can get in after school. The following morning, Jackie walked right in, carrying a pair of scissors in her pocket. "I wanted to stab him, but he woke up before I could get to him. He grabbed the scissors from me and we started fighting. I slapped him and punched him in the face. He kept shouting at the top of his lungs, 'You're crazy. I don't want to see you no more.'"

Jackie ran into the kitchen to get a knife. George followed and tried to wrest the knife from her. They rolled and wrestled into the living room where he had almost succeeded when the television fell on him.

Jackie says, "I thought, 'Oh, my God, he's hurt.' I rushed to help him. He got up, shaking his head and pushed me away. I was so hurt. Why does he always push me away? I rushed back into the kitchen for another knife."

Meanwhile, George grabbed the phone and called his grandmother. She asked to talk to Jackie. Jackie held the knife tight with one hand and reached for the receiver with the other. George's grandmother told Jackie to leave George alone.

George's grandmother was able to calm Jackie down. She even dropped the knife and sat cross-legged on the floor, holding her head in her hands. Very carefully, George reached for the knife and took it to the kitchen where it belonged. While there, he called Jackie's mother and sister, who rushed right over to take her home.

Once Jackie was safely home, her mother helped her into bed and went off to make coffee. Jackie quickly got up, dressed, and jumped out her window. She went straight back to George. She knocked on the door.

He opened the door a crack to see if she had another knife. Jackie said, "I want to talk to you. AND LISTEN TO ME!"

Jackie was crying. George asked her to go home and he promised to call her later. Once home, Jackie sat by the phone for three hours before she decided that another visit to George's apartment was necessary.

"I pounded on George's front door so hard that my knuckles began to bleed. I wanted to knock the door down, but it was too hard. When I knocked louder and louder, he played his radio louder and louder. My friends who live in the building came by and asked me what was wrong. I said, 'Nothing, just leave!' I went downstairs and waited outside. I told *everybody* on the block what happened. I'm like that. I tell everybody my problems, but now I know better. I could see that people started talking about me. That made things worse."

Three hours later George came out of his house all dressed up. He met one of his friends, a girl, and he hugged her right in front of Jackie.

Jackie said, "What are you trying to do, get me jealous? It's not working." She started cursing at him as he left with his friend.

For four days Jackie sat looking out her window, four days in a row doing nothing but looking. Whenever anyone passed by, she called, "Have you seen George? Have you seen him with a girl?" But no one had seen him.

Jackie refused to eat. "I was sick, throwing up green stuff. I was crying all the time. I didn't go outside. I didn't do nothing. I wasn't thinking about the baby. All I could think about was George."

One afternoon, George's mother passed by her window. She asked Jackie if her mother was home. George's and Jackie's mothers had a summit meeting to end all summit meetings. They were very polite, very pleasant. They talked about everything: Jackie's temper and jealousy, George's unreliability and unkept promises. Both mothers resolved to talk to their children.

Jackie says, "Afterwards, George's mother talked to him. He promised to change. He said he was not mad at me no more."

Once George called Jackie, everything went back to the way it was before the knife incident. A few days later, Jackie spent the evening with George and his family. They watched TV and she cooked his dinner. When she became tired, she lay down on the sofa. After a *Miami Vice* rerun, George wanted to be alone. Jackie peacefully succumbed to his wishes. She walked to the door and George gallantly opened it for her. As she walked down the stairs, he called after her softly, "No more fights." Jackie was not sure what he meant by that.

By Jackie's last month there were appointments with Sylvie every week. The couple faithfully attended Lamaze classes and took a tour of the maternity ward. During her last visit to the clinic Jackie peeked into Mrs. Joseph's office. "Well, well, well. Look at you! You're just about ready," the coordinator said to her.

Jackie opened wide her jacket to model her pregnancy. "Yep, Sylvie says that my baby will come any day now. I'm so excited."

Mrs. Joseph stood up and gave Jackie a big hug. Jackie hugged back and turned to leave. Not so fast! "Jackie, when your baby is born, are you going to use birth control?" Mrs. Joseph held onto Jackie's shoulders deliberately to emphasize her seriousness.

"I already talked to Sylvie about the pill."

"That's good. Remember what I always say, 'A pill a day keeps the next baby away.'"

Jackie smiled.

Mrs. Joseph was not finished. She rapped her wooden desk with her fist. *Knock. Knock. Knock.* "These knocks are to remind you to take your pill every night before you go to bed. After your baby is born, I want you to think of Mrs. Joseph under your bed, knocking. I'm right under your bed!" *Knock. Knock.*

Mrs. Joseph, while amicable, was deadly serious. She continued, "Give me a break! You don't need that next baby. So remember my knocking."

Jackie crossed her heart, promised faithfully to listen to Mrs. Joseph, and raced off to George who was in the waiting room.

Labor pains began at five o'clock while Jackie was home alone watching TV. "I started getting these pains in my stomach. It didn't hurt that much, it was a little like getting my period. But they didn't go away. In fact, they got stronger and stronger. I thought, 'Oh, my God, I better call George.'"

George, his mother, his aunt, and his little sister rushed to Jackie's apartment. Jackie's mother and father arrived home to find George running around the house screaming, "Oh, my God, she's having the baby already!"

"My mother started timing me. George was so excited. That made me feel good in spite of the pains. Then we drove down the street to the hospital.

"George didn't know what to do in the labor room. The midwife told him to hold my head while I pushed. Do you know what he did? He dropped my head. Three times!

"I pushed some more and after twenty-five minutes our baby—a girl—came out. When George saw her coming, especially with all that red stuff, how you call it, the placenta, he shouted, 'Oh, my God, I've never seen this before!' He was shocked. I wasn't at all scared. I wasn't shocked. Sylvie taught me all about it.

"We named her Crystal. I was happy she was a girl. George says that he likes girls better than boys even though he said that he wanted a son. He likes her—a lot. I stayed in the hospital for three days. I had a bunch of visitors and got lots of flowers. George gave me roses and all kinds of things."

Once Jackie and Crystal were home with her family, Jackie found

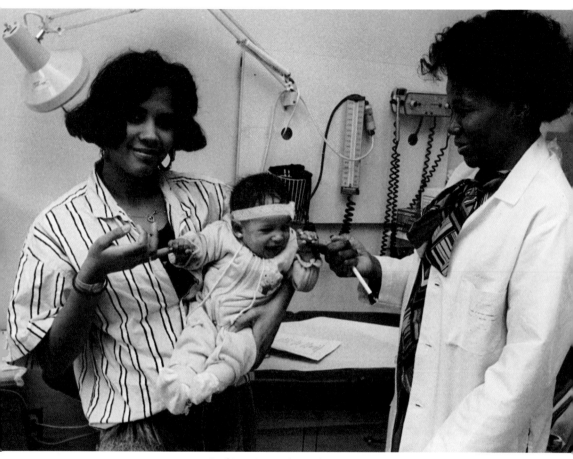

Jackie, Crystal, and Mrs. Joseph

that it was not hard being a mom. "Everyone helps me. When the baby gets up in the middle of the night and cries, I don't mind getting up. It doesn't matter what time she gets up, I love to feed her.

"George is a good father. He's not so good as a boyfriend, but he's better than he was. I pick up milk for the baby at the hospital from the WIC program (a government nutritional program for women, infants, and children). George pays for everything else. He gives her the milk, but he won't bathe her or change her diapers. I do all of that. It's my baby. Boys are funny. We girls have to do everything. When Crystal cries in the middle of the night, George never wakes up to give her milk. I do it all the time, but I don't mind. We still argue, but not as much as before. I'm not as jealous as I was. If he wants to be with me, he can. If he don't, he can leave. He don't dare look at other girls. Not with me. He never did. I know that now."

Four Months Later

Crystal is four months old. George and Jackie are getting along much better these days. Jackie must have forgotten that Mrs. Joseph was under her bed knocking to remind her to take the pill. Jackie is pregnant again.

A lecture on contraceptives

19

"I Thought It Would Be Fun to Have a Baby"

BY LATE morning the adolescent clinic is charged with activity. Maude Joseph helps weigh an infant, all the while instructing the teenagers who gather to watch her. A fourteen-year-old mother holding her six-month-old daughter prances down the hall. Mrs. Joseph spots her. "How's your baby doing? Did you give her the pink medicine?"

"How did you know about that?" the teen asks, surprised that the director knows about a medication prescribed the previous night.

"Ah, Big Sister is watching you," Mrs. Joseph says as she takes the baby in her arms. "You took your baby to the emergency room last night. I know all about it."

Mrs. Joseph's first responsibility each morning is to review the previous night's emergency and maternity lists. "If I see the name of one of my girls on the emergency room list, I want to know why. When she comes in for a checkup, I talk to her about it. My girls love that. They know that there are knowledgeable adults here who care about their well being. And we do. Here, we all do."

Mrs. Joseph has four sons and one grandson. No girls. "My daughters are NBH (North Bronx Hospital) girls. I tell them that they are in my 'Daughters' Club.'"

Mrs. Joseph's "girls" are constantly on her mind. "I think about them all the time. At night, when I'm at home doing the dishes, I plan things for the program. Perhaps the running water has some effect on my psyche because ideas always spout out. I keep a pad and pen handy so that I can jot them down."

In an alcove between examination rooms, a lecture, video, and demonstration about contraceptives is in progress. Nine pregnant teenagers, but no fathers-to-be, watch attentively. A childbirth educator shows a video detailing various kinds of contraception. Afterward she asks, "Any questions? Anything at all?"

No questions.

She gathers her props: condoms, foam, and a diaphragm, as the girls begin to leave.

"Don't go away! Don't go away!" a second educator calls out as she scurries to a chair next to the video screen. Reaching into a large purple beach bag, she pulls out a much-used beige pillow, shaped like a bosom, brown protruding nipple included. "I want to talk to you about the advantages of breast-feeding. Don't go away! Don't go away!" she pleads, "I have a wonderful video. This is really a good thing."

For some reason the girls disappear and in their place the no-where-to-be-found, wide-eyed fathers miraculously materialize. The boys, who were not particularly interested in a demonstration about contraceptives, appear to be somewhat turned on to a video on breast-feeding.

Amused by the swap, the educator doesn't miss a beat. She begins her spiel while the boys politely wait for the video.

Inside the examining room, thirteen-year-old Nancy watches Dr. Quijano examine her daughter.

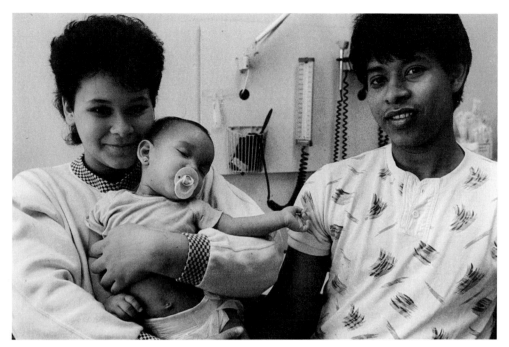

Nancy, Erica, and Hector

Nancy, 13

Nancy is a short, chubby girl with creamy skin, dimples, and an aura of innocence that belies her situation. At age eleven Nancy would often watch for the attractive twenty-three-year-old construction worker who lived across the street. She'd lower her eyes, shyly saying, "Hi." He, too, looked forward to seeing her. Five months later, she and Hector were having sex.

"It was scary to have sex at first, but afterwards it became very exciting," she says. "Sex is not anything to be sad about, it is something to enjoy. I never thought about such things as babies and contraceptives when I was eleven.

"I live with my grandmother. My mother was a teenager when she had me, but she was too young to take care of me. She lives in an apartment upstairs. We never got along.

"My boyfriend, Hector, and I were together all the time. That caused family problems, big family problems. My grandmother said that he was too old for me. But by that time, I was twelve! We ran away to a cheap motel and lived there for a while. One day, without any warning, the cops arrived. Hector was arrested for 'corrupting a minor' and I was put into a foster home. You could say I lived a wild life. After a while I moved back to my grandmother's house. Hector got out of jail and we started seeing each other again. By then I knew all about birth control, but I never used it. I wanted a baby. I thought it would be fun to have a baby! Pretty clothes, toys, my child by my side as I walked down the street.

"When I became pregnant, Hector and I were ecstatic. My grandmother wanted me to get an abortion, but Hector would not go along with that at all. Before the baby was born, we spent all our money on things for her: a crib, a stroller, a bathing area, clothes, and toys. Tons of toys. It was fun. As my due date approached, we had no money for our own place so Hector moved in with my grandmother and me. They fought all the time. Eventually, she threw him out of our apartment.

"Erica was born by C section because the doctor said my cervix was too small for me to deliver a baby. The delivery was easier than I thought it would be. They just put me to sleep and when I woke up, I was a mother.

"Afterwards all hell broke out. Suddenly I was faced with so many responsibilities. I was up every night because Erica kept crying. I couldn't stand the crying, day in and day out. I needed to sleep, but I couldn't.

"Even worse than the crying was money. I needed lots of it. One week, I didn't have enough money to buy food for Erica. And she needed so many Pampers. I asked my family to help pay for the baby's food and Pampers. They were furious at me for having the child in the first place and they didn't want to help me out. But they did. What choice did they have? Hector gave me as much money as he could, but he doesn't make very much.

"When my friends dropped by to invite me to a party, I'd ask my

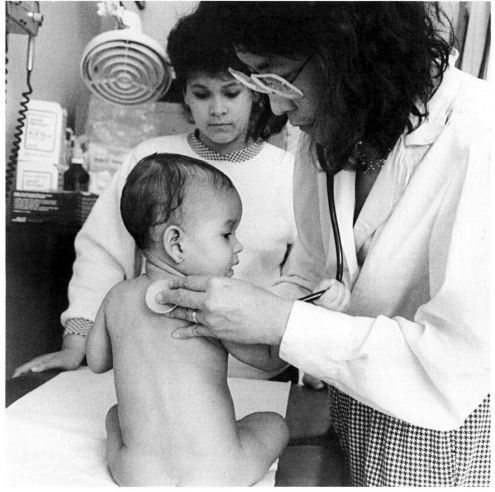

Dr. Emelyn Quijano examines Nancy's daughter, Erica

grandmother to take care of the baby. Sometimes she said 'No,' and I felt left out and became upset.

"The best part of my day is when I go to the clinic to be with Dr. Quijano. She teaches me how to take care of my baby.

"I visit Hector every weekend in a room that he rents nearby. I bring Erica with me. I never leave my baby overnight."

Nancy learned to take the pill, but she thought it was making her fat. Then, when she heard a report on TV linking breast cancer and the pill, she said, "Forget it." Dr. Quijano explained that she was very unlikely to get cancer from the low hormone dose in her pill, but Nancy is still afraid to risk it.

"I thought about using a diaphragm, but that didn't work out. Hector uses condoms, but I'm having a little trouble with him about using them."

Before Nancy became pregnant she constantly went out with Hector. Now she must stay at home with the baby. Hector continues to go out whenever he wants. That infuriates Nancy. "You see what happened," Nancy complains to him. "You said you were going to help me take care of Erica. You said we would be together always. You said you wouldn't go out on the streets."

Hector tries to help out. When he's not at work, he accompanies Nancy and Erica to the clinic to learn how to take care of the baby.

"Now I'm pregnant again. I have a big decision to make. I don't like abortion. What I hear about it is disgusting. But I have too many problems with Erica. If I have another child, it's going to be worse. Erica doesn't suffer, but if another baby comes along, there won't be enough of me to give to both of them. The future of my baby is in my hands. I'm thirteen years old and never finished school. How am I going to educate Erica?"

Dr. Quijano's next appointment is with Melissa Figueroa. Like Nancy, Melissa's appearance is young, shy, and innocent. Unlike Nancy, Melissa planned for her future. But then, Melissa is older.

Melissa Figueroa, 15

Melissa's husband was her first boyfriend. "I'd been with him for two and a half years and I wanted to have a baby. He wanted one, too. If we had a baby he promised that he would share the responsibility. I got pregnant on purpose. My boyfriend and I were living together at the time. When I told my mother that I wanted to have a baby, she said that was a big responsibility. But she gave me the green light as long as I felt that I was ready for it.

"My boyfriend was really nice when I was pregnant. I used to wake him up in the middle of the night to go to the store for me. He'd say, 'Oh, please, can't you wait till tomorrow?' and I'd say, 'No! No, I want it now.' He would actually get up and go to the store for me.

"Once I became pregnant, I got serious. I started thinking that if I wanted to live a good life, I had to go to college and get a good job. My husband may not be there for the rest of my life. If something happens to him, or if we break up, I don't want to go on welfare. My mother is on welfare and I don't want that. I want to work and do something for myself."

During Melissa's pregnancy she went to school at night and in the summertime. She was able to skip an entire grade.

"My delivery was hard and long. I tried to deal with the pain. My boyfriend and my mother were in the room. He was supportive. He rubbed my head and my belly. And my mother did, too.

"A few months after the birth, we got married. My husband enrolled at the police academy.

"I expected it to be hard, but not this hard. When the baby cries at night, I'm the one who gets up. I'm tired all the time. When I don't feel well, my husband takes over. He promised me that he would do that, and he kept his promise.

"I'm glad I have my baby, but if I had the chance to do it all over again, I don't think I would do it."

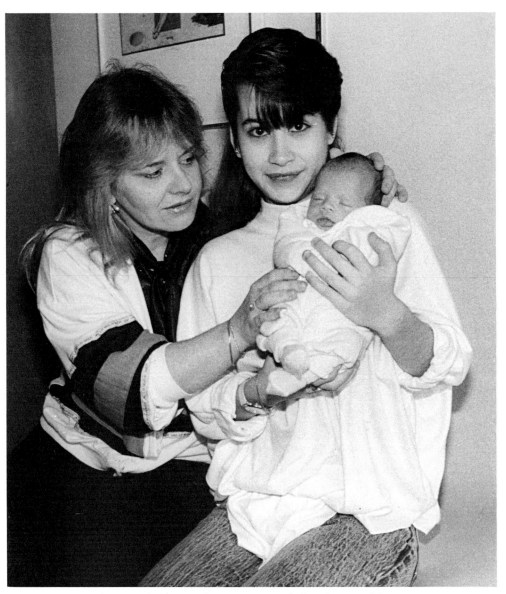

Melissa with her mother, Doris, and daughter, Ashley

20

"Something I'm Going to Have to Live With"

Melissa, 15

THERE is another Melissa, a petite, freckle-faced teenager with tousled blond hair. Boys have not been a positive influence in her life. Some of them misinterpreted her sweet, shy disposition which made her a passive, easy mark and tried to take advantage of her.

Wearing designer jeans she sits beside her equally blond mother, Doris, in the waiting room at the Adolescent Clinic. Doris moved to the States from Germany when she married an American. Once she and her husband divorced, Doris became determined to provide a good life for herself and for her children. Although she worked at a low-paying job, she maintained an attractive, clean apartment and provided emotional support and love for Melissa and her younger brother. Her dream, though, was to give her children more. She enrolled in classes at night in order to get a diploma and a better job.

Although Melissa has an extremely close and loving relationship with both her mother and brother, her life has been tough. "I caught my first boyfriend, a high school football player, sneaking around with my best friend. Some best friend! I got rid of both of them. After spending a lonely summer without anyone special in my life, along came my second boyfriend, Leo (name and identity changed), Mr. Make-it-all-sound-good."

Doris says, "I didn't like Leo. I didn't trust him. I allowed him in my house only so I could keep an eye on him when he was with my daughter."

For weeks Leo hung out at Melissa's house from morning till nighttime. Doris says, "They were spending too much time together. He was at my house every day. I wanted to be alone with my kids. I wanted Melissa to date many boys. I was afraid that spending time with one guy would lead to trouble. Perhaps I should have insisted. I saw it coming.

"One day I asked Leo point blank: 'Doesn't your mother worry about you? Doesn't she call to see how you are?'

"He said, 'No, she don't care what I do.'

"I felt sorry for him. I resolved to overcome my apprehensions and treat him like he was one of my own."

Once Leo became part of the family, his behavior changed. He became rough with Melissa. One night he grabbed her by the neck. Another night he kicked her when she walked ahead of him. When Melissa complained, he laughed, saying that he was only fooling around.

Then, in school, in front of a group of their friends, he punched her. When he hit her in school, her friends started to scream at him. Her friend's boyfriend hit him. They got into a fight.

After the punching incident, Doris begged Melissa to break up with Leo. "Get rid of him," she pleaded. Melissa would not listen. She didn't want to be the only one in her crowd without a boyfriend.

Meanwhile, the only thing Melissa's friends talked about was sex. They talked about it incessantly, endlessly. Melissa became curious. "Leo pressed me, saying, 'Oh, this is good for you. You'll like it. . . .' And me, like a dummy, listened. I listened to my friends and I listened to Leo. I thought, 'I'm fifteen, I may as well go along with it.' After school, we went to his house. That's where we did it."

As soon as they became intimate, everything had to be his way. "Leo was into a power thing. When I expressed an opinion, he became vicious."

Late one night, in Melissa's apartment, he hit her, hard. She pulled away from him and raced into the bathroom. He followed, threatening, cursing, and finally kicking the bathroom door in. Doris, awakened by the furor, jumped out of bed, screaming, "Get out of my house and never come back." Submissively, Leo left the house, without causing more commotion.

Two days later, he reappeared. He returned with promises to Melissa that he would work out his problems. "Everything will be better than before," he vowed, head low, reaching for both her hands.

"I need some time," she told him. Leo backed off and did not see Melissa for a number of weeks.

Invariably, since they lived in the same neighborhood, Melissa eventually saw Leo. "Will you still be with me? Will you be my girl?" he begged.

"I'm willing to see you and I'm willing to go out with you, but only as friends. No sex!"

Leo tried to convince Melissa to become his girlfriend again, but she refused. Since he had no other choice, Leo agreed to the new relationship: just friends. They made a date to go to the movies that night.

Then, at Leo's house after the movies, he changed the ground rules. "For a little thing, he's pretty strong. He held me down and I couldn't get away from him. He forced me to have sex with him. I didn't want that."

After the date rape, Melissa wanted never to see his face again.

Then she began to worry. "What if I have a disease? What if I'm pregnant?" Everything had happened so fast. Obviously, Leo had not been concerned about birth control.

There was no indication that Melissa was pregnant. Her period came at regular monthly intervals and she felt no morning sickness or nausea. Still, she worried.

"I didn't need any more complications in my life. I went to a clinic and took a pregnancy test just to make sure. When the test came back negative, I was relieved. I didn't want to have to explain anything to my mother.

"About sixteen weeks after I broke up with Leo, I felt little bumps inside my stomach. I thought they were gas pains. A little later I noticed that my bellybutton started to stick out. My doctor said it was a hernia. It would have to be taken out with surgery. Before my operation a friend told me about the teen clinic at the hospital. I decided to double-check my hernia. When I saw the pediatrician, Dr. Quijano, she had doubts about my hernia." The doctor took Melissa's urine for a pregnancy test and it came back positive.

Dr. Quijano returned to the examination room with the results of the test. "Are you sure? Check again," Melissa pleaded. The doctor checked again with a blood test. Positive.

An internal exam confirmed a thirty-one week pregnancy. It was too late for an abortion and, besides, Melissa didn't believe in that as an option. Her only choices were to carry the pregnancy to term and keep the child or give it up for adoption.

No matter what the decision was, Doris was going to find out about the pregnancy. How could Melissa tell her mother, who was sitting anxiously in the waiting room? Dr. Quijano says, "Melissa thought that she was up against the whole world. At this point I was the most knowledgeable person in her life to help her to face the situation."

Totally freaked out, Melissa stared blankly at the doctor. It took a while for everything to sink in. "I was shocked. I thought, *'His kid?'* After everything he did to me and now I'm having his kid?"

Dr. Quijano tried to give Melissa the self-confidence she needed to face her mother. The doctor held her hands and said, "You really cannot hide this anymore. I know that you are scared to tell your mother, but I am here to help you. She will probably cry, but we'll face it together."

Without letting go of her doctor's hands, Melissa looked up at her and nodded. Then Dr. Quijano called the front desk to invite Doris into the examination room.

"Is it a hernia?" Doris asked as she entered the room.

"No," the doctor answered."

"What do you mean? Tell me—tell me. She's pregnant. Right?"

Melissa couldn't look at her mother. Instead, she looked down at her shoes and cried.

"Whose is it?" her mother demanded and mentioned every fellow Melissa ever went out with, except one.

"I kept shaking my head no, no, no . . ."

Finally, she said, "Oh, no, it can't be."

"Yeah, him."

Everything was happening so fast. Melissa wanted to finish school and then find a good job. She wasn't ready to become a mother. "Maybe if I could find a good home for the baby," Melissa reasoned. "Give it life, then go on with mine."

Melissa scarcely had time for counseling. At her first prenatal checkup with Sylvie, she told the midwife that she definitely wanted to give the baby up for adoption. Sylvie said, "We'll do whatever you say. But it's a big decision. Take your time and think it over. You have at least a month to decide."

"I made my decision. I won't change my mind," Melissa declared firmly.

An appointment was set up with the Spence–Chapin adoption agency for the second of September. "I felt strongly that I needed to finish high school, go to college, and then have kids. I'll give my future kids what I can't give to this baby. I kept saying to myself, 'I'm gonna do this. I'm gonna do this . . . I know I can leave the hospital . . . I know that the baby will be safe . . . I know I won't feel hurt.'"

After the positive diagnosis, Melissa felt "gas pains" again. This time she understood that they were little kicks inside her. She asked her mother if she wanted to feel it, but her mother didn't want to.

Caught between being a mother and a future grandmother, Doris was in a quandary. "If I told her to keep the baby, she would throw it back at me later. I don't want her to say, 'My life is miserable and messed up because of you.'

"Still, deep down inside, I was hoping that she would change her mind. A neighbor suggested that I adopt the baby myself. I would have liked to, but then Melissa would have to move out. It's not considered advisable for the birth mother to live with the baby. Mostly, I kept my mouth shut."

Every once in a while, though, Doris could not keep quiet. She never actually told her daughter what to do, but she hinted. "I know you're strong. You're stronger than you think," she said.

No reply.

Melissa's younger brother did more than hint. "Someday you will be walking in a mall and your own daughter might be right in front of you and you won't even know it. Can you live with that, Melissa?"

"That's something I'm going to have to live with."

A week later when Melissa was in her thirty-second week, she went into premature labor. Melissa and her mother rushed to the hospital.

Doris says, "We were hoping it would be Sylvie who would deliver her. The midwives are all very nice, but Sylvie took care of her once we learned about the pregnancy. I was crossing my fingers that she would be the one to deliver the baby. Our prayers were answered, at least for the time being." When Sylvie arrived for delivery room duty, she found Melissa in labor. Once again, Sylvie asked Melissa what she wanted to do about the baby. "Melissie, you have to tell me what you want me to do? Do you want me to take the baby away immediately so that you don't see it? I have to know now."

Melissa held firmly to her decision. "As much as it's going to hurt me, just take it away, don't show it to me at all." Doris, still hoping that her daughter would hear the baby cry and change her mind, was disappointed by the steadfast reply.

Hospitals' procedures vary in policy and routine. At North Central Bronx a baby is usually delivered in a labor room that looks like a private room with a bed, chairs, pictures on the wall, and a bathroom. If there are complications, for example, a premature delivery or a baby under stress, the mother gives birth in a delivery room that looks like an operating room with an OR table, a big light, and lots of machinery in case emergencies arise.

Since Melissa's baby would be two months premature, she was moved into the delivery room. A pediatrician had to be present during the delivery because some premature babies are so small that their lungs might not be developed enough to function on their own.

"Labor was rough, twenty-eight hours of pure pain. Sylvie stayed as long as she could but then another midwife took over. Then another. I went through two shifts of midwives. I saw the same shift of nurses twice."

When Sylvie returned to the hospital for her second shift, she learned that Melissa was still in labor. Sylvie says, "When I arrived, Melissa was in a lot of pain. It took some time before the baby girl came out kicking. It was a vigorous birth. That baby didn't need any help at all. For a preemie, she appeared quite healthy. She let out a strong, hearty yowl. I cut the cord and gave the baby to the pediatrician. After he examined her and declared her healthy, he gave the baby back to me."

Doris says, "Everyone was crying. When I saw the baby, it broke my heart."

Melissa was afraid to look at the crying newborn. "Do you want to hold it?" she asked her mother.

Doris says that she wanted to hold her so badly, but at the same time, she was afraid to love her too much.

Then, hearing the baby's cry, Melissa wavered and asked to see the baby. "I looked at this tiny infant and I thought, 'My God, this is my kid. I gave life to her.'

"I looked up at Sylvie. 'Can I touch her?'

"Sylvie put the baby on my chest. From that second on, I knew that I couldn't let her go.

"I thought, 'Wait a minute, what am I doing? She's mine. I can't give her away!' I looked over to my mother, who was crying. 'Mom? We . . . we . . . can . . . work this out, right? I can't give her away.'

"I was sobbing, telling all the people in the room, 'She was inside of me. I gave her life. Give her up? Am I crazy? I can't do that.' I fell in love with her."

Because everything had happened so quickly, Melissa had not called the adoption agency. Had the situation gone as originally planned, she would have left the baby at the hospital and returned home alone. The adoption agency would then take the baby to a foster home and, once the surrender papers were signed, to her new family. That was no longer conceivable.

Premature births can often require months of intensive medical care. But Melissa's baby, Ashley, weighed over five pounds at birth and was very healthy. She was lucky. After three days, Melissa, her mother, and her brother triumphantly brought Ashley home. Doris says, "That was our happiest day."

After a few weeks, Melissa went through some changes. She became depressed. She was tired all the time, but rarely slept. Instead, she lay in bed thinking about her future.

"Mom," she cried a month after the baby came home, "I'm fifteen and my life is already messed up. It's hard to go to school and take care of a baby. I can't go out with my friends anymore. There's nothing that I can do that a fifteen-year-old does. My life is over."

Doris comforted Melissa, "Your life is not over. You are more fortunate than girls who don't have anyone to help them. I'm willing to help work things out. You go to school during the day and I'll go to school at night. We'll both get diplomas and better jobs. We'll be a team. And you will graduate like all the other girls your age. Before you know it, the time will go by so quick."

21

"If You Live on My Block
You Have Babies"

"ONE baby!" Mrs. Joseph is standing in front of her office talking to a fourteen-year-old. "You came to me pregnant so I would accept you into my Daughters' Club. But you don't need another baby." The teenager, struggling to hold her squirming son, appears to be listening.

In order to ensure a healthy delivery and safe prenatal care, Mrs. Joseph will go along with a teenager who decides to keep her child. "But after that, I want each of them to try their best not to have another baby.

"I constantly talk to them about birth control and they understand what I'm talking about. But still they get pregnant." Mrs. Joseph returns to her office and sits down at her desk, shaking her head. "I wish they would never have that second baby. I want them to pick up their lives, learn skills, and do positive things for themselves and for their babies."

"If you live on my block, you have babies," says Charlene Rodriguez, a delicate, slender teenager who patiently sits in the waiting room until Sylvie calls her name. Charlene's neat ponytail is perched high on her head. Thin black liner shapes her eyes. In her baby-blue running pants and white sweater emblazoned with a gold "A," it is easy to overlook that she is pregnant, but resting on her lap, like an oversized basketball, is the perfectly rounded shape of an eight-month pregnancy.

Charlene, 16

When Charlene was fourteen she became pregnant. "My boyfriend, Charley, and I use birth control, foam, but I became pregnant anyway. We wanted to have the baby, but we were afraid about how our parents would react. I decided to have an abortion.

"I couldn't tell my mother and father, but I could confide in my aunt. She took me to a clinic where I had an abortion. Charley came with us. He was there for me through the entire ordeal.

"When I went into the room and saw all the machines, I panicked. I wondered, 'Would I wake up?' I didn't want to go through with it. But I felt that I had to because I didn't know how my mother would react to my pregnancy. Afterwards, I stayed at my aunt's house for a few days. Once it was done, I was sad. I wondered how it would have looked. How my mother and father would have reacted if I had kept the baby. Sometimes I still wonder if it was a girl or a boy."

When Charlene's mother finally found out about the abortion, she was furious that she had not been informed. She told her daughter that she should have come to her, trusted her.

Like so many other young couples, Charlene and Charley were neighbors. At first they didn't get along. Later he became interested in her. When he spied her walking down the street, he would rush over to talk to her. Charlene paid no attention to him. Eventually, Charley became very friendly with the other members of Charlene's family. Charlene's mother in particular liked him and took him with her to parties. Charley and Charlene's mother became confi-

Charlene with Sylvie

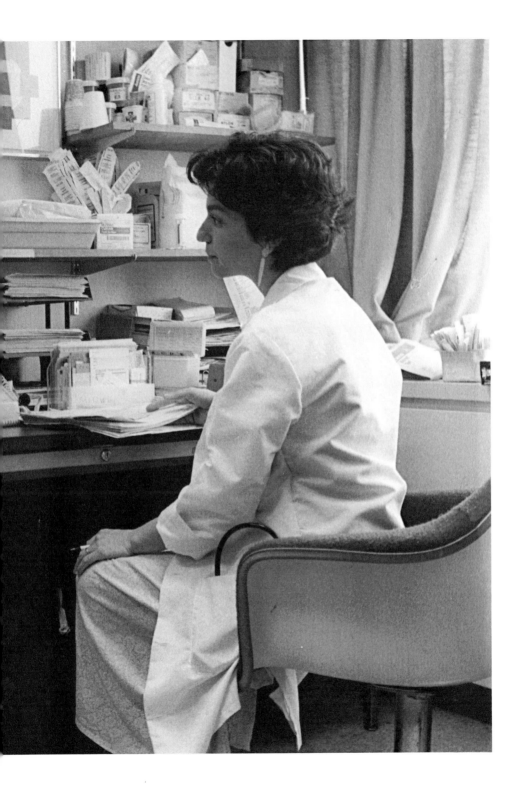

dants. In fact, he admitted his love for Charlene to her mother before finding the courage to tell Charlene herself.

When Charlene learned that she had an admirer, she said, "Oh, my God, what am I going to do?" By this time she had become very attracted to Charley, but she didn't want him to know about it. She was thirteen.

Charley courted Charlene by buying gifts, such as combs, clothes, and things like that. Though she liked him, her mother warned Charlene not to get too close. "Don't worry," Charlene said, "we're just friends." But actually by this time, Charlene was falling in love with him and debating whether or not to sleep with him.

"Where sex was concerned, I had a big conflict. I was attracted to Charley and curious about sex. But I heard so many stories about guys taking advantage of girls and leaving them flat. I thought, 'If I have sex with him, will he leave me? What happens afterwards?'

"Finally, since I was only thirteen, I decided that I was not ready to have sex. When I told him, he was very understanding. He eased off. For four months we went to the movies and to parties. We became closer and closer, and I trusted him more and more. I was so happy."

Once again, after an evening filled with laughing and dancing, Charley asked Charlene to have sex with him. "No, no. I'm scared. I'm scared you might leave me," she said.

"That would never happen," Charley promised.

"So we had sex and he never left me and we're still together to this day. He's the only boyfriend I've ever had. He's with me every day. I'm lucky."

When Charlene became pregnant the second time, her father cautioned her to keep this one, incorrectly explaining that another abortion "would mess up her insides."

Once the decision was made to keep the baby, practical plans were formulated. Charlene's mother volunteered to take care of the baby so that she will be able to return to school. Baby furniture, clothes, and toys are being bought and borrowed. "I'm happy that

I'm pregnant, but I wish I had waited. Later I would be able to give my baby more things."

Oddly, family and friends haven't talked about the actual act of having a baby, even though there were many questions Charlene needed answered. The only place where she felt comfortable asking questions was at the clinic. "The scary part is having it. I wonder about the labor pains. No one at my house would tell me about it. When I came here and talked to Sylvie, she answered every question. I don't know what I would do without Sylvie. Charley says that the scariest part for him also is the labor. He don't want to look at it come out. I think Charley should talk to Sylvie."

Before her pregnancy Charlene, 5'4", weighed eighty-five pounds. Now she's almost 118. During an earlier prenatal checkup Sylvie told her that a pregnant woman should gain twenty-five to thirty pounds in order to have a healthy baby. "I was worried about becoming fat. It was weird when my body started swelling up. Charley says he likes me better this way. He likes me bigger than I was. I get no morning sickness, but sometimes I get tired. I don't smoke, drink, and have never taken drugs. Charley smokes cigarettes, that's all.

"With two exceptions, all of my friends have babies. The two that don't seem to be having much more fun than the rest of us. When the rest of us hang out, all we ever talk about is what we can give our babies. Some of my friends don't have their babies' fathers around. They tell me how lucky I am because my boyfriend is still with me. Of my five best girlfriends who are pregnant or have babies, three still have the same boyfriends—but they play around with other girls. My boyfriend does not play around.

"Right now Charley is living with his family. In the future we will get married and have our own apartment. I want to wear a beautiful white gown at a big wedding—a big one."

Finale

P.S. Sylvie is pregnant. She and her husband are very excited about their carefully planned third child.

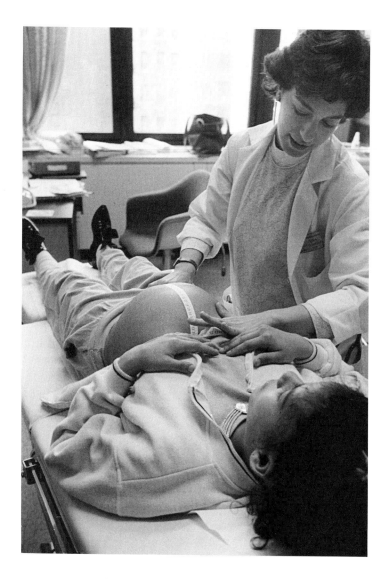

Glossary

ABORTION: the termination of a pregnancy either voluntary or involuntary.

AMNIOTIC FLUID: a fluid which surrounds the fetus in the uterus.

ANEMIA: any condition in which the number of red blood cells, the amount of hemoglobin, and the volume of packed red blood cells are less than normal. Anemia is frequently manifested by pallor of the skin and mucous membranes, shortness of breath, palpitations of the heart, lack of usual energy, etc.

ANESTHESIA: total loss of sensation in a part or in the entire body generally induced by the administration of a drug.

BIOPSY: the process of removing tissue from living patients for diagnostic examination.

CESAREAN (C SECTION): the operation by which a fetus is taken from the uterus by cutting through the walls of the abdomen and uterus (supposedly performed at the birth of Julius Caesar).

CERVIX: the neck of the uterus that dilates just before childbirth.

CONTRACEPTION: the prevention of conception by deliberate methods.

CONTRACTION: the change of a muscle by which it becomes thickened and shortened.

CURETTAGE: a scraping of the interior of the uterus for the removal of a pregnancy or abnormal tissues.

CURETTAGE, SUCTION: the aspiration of uterine contents.

CURETTE: an instrument in the form of a loop, ring, or scoop, with sharpened edges, attached to a rod-shaped handle, used to scrape the interior of a cavity for the removal of new growths or altered tissues.

DILATION: the act of stretching the cervix.

DILATION AND CURETTAGE (D & C): The stretching and scraping of the inside of the uterus for various medical reasons. With most first-trimester abortions, this is followed by suction.

DILATION AND EVACUATION (D & E): (most) second trimester abortions. The stretching and removal of the pregnancy from of the uterus. This procedure requires more suction than a first-trimester abortion.

EMBRYO: an organism in the earlier stages of development.

EVACUATION: the use of a vacuum or a very low pressure in order to empty the uterus of fetal tissues.

FETUS: the product of conception from the end of the eighth week to the moment of birth.

GENERAL ANESTHESIA: anesthesia in which the patient is totally asleep during the procedure.

GYNECOLOGIST: a medical doctor who deals with the functions and diseases peculiar to women.

GYNECOLOGY: the branch of medicine which has to do with the diseases peculiar to women, primarily those of the genital tract, as well as female endocrinology and reproductive physiology.

LAMAZE: a method of natural childbirth using breathing and exercise techniques in which the parents are able to participate and aid in the birth of the child.

LAMINARIA: seaweed-like substance that is inserted into the cervix to help stretch it.

LOCAL ANESTHESIA: anesthesia confined to a limited part of the body. The patient is awake during the procedure but the area being operated on is without feeling.

MIDWIFE: a person who attends women during a healthy pregnancy and delivery.

MIDWIFERY: the practice and art of assisting women in childbirth.

MISCARRIAGE: the expulsion of the product of conception early in the pregnancy.

PAP SMEAR: a screening test for cervical cancer.

PARACERVICAL BLOCK: a method of local anesthesia.

PEDIATRICIAN: a physician who specializes in the diseases of children.

PERFORATED UTERUS: when the womb is pierced with one or more holes.

PERINEUM: the wall between the vagina and the anus.

PLACENTA: supporting tissue for the fetus to enable it to feed, breathe, and eliminate waste products.

PRENATAL: previous to birth.

PREMATURE: occurring before the usual or expected time.

SALINE ABORTION: method to induce abortion. The procedure is usually performed in a hospital. A hypertonic solution is put into the uterus via a needle in the abdomen. The medication will produce labor and the fetus will be passed.

SONOGRAM: an ultrasound picture without radiation.

TRIMESTER: One-third of the length of a pregnancy. First trimester—between one and thirteen weeks. Second trimester—between thirteen and twenty-eight weeks. Third trimester—between twenty-eight and forty weeks.

UMBILICAL CORD: a cord connecting the embryo or fetus with the placenta of the mother and transmitting nourishment from the mother.

UTERUS: the womb.

VAGINA: the genital canal in the female, extending from the uterus to the vulva.

VULVA: the external female genitalia.

WOMB: the uterus.

Note: most definitions are from the 22nd edition of Stedman's Medical Dictionary *and* The American College Dictionary.

Afterword

If you think you are pregnant and need help, look in the Yellow Pages under "Pregnancy." You will find listings for various services. When you call them, be sure to ask if they discuss all options, including adoption, abortion, and keeping your baby, and if they will not answer this question, call another organization.